WHEN YOU ARE STUCK IN A RUT & NEED A MOTIVATIONAL KICK IN THE BUTT, READ THIS BOOK!

WHEN YOU ARE STUCK IN A RUT & NEED A MOTIVATIONAL KICK IN THE BUTT, READ THIS BOOK!

It Just Might Save Your Life! Volume 2

BY JENNIFER NICOLE LEE
& SPECIAL CONTRIBUTING AUTHORS

Medical Disclaimer

The information in this work is in no way intended as medical advice or as a substitute for medical counseling. This publication contains the opinions and ideas of its author. It is intended to provide helpful and informative material on the subjects addressed in the publication. It is sold with the understanding that the author and publisher are not engaged in rendering medical, health, psychological, or any other kind of personal professional services in the book. If the reader requires personal medical, health, or other assistance or advice, a competent professional should be consulted. The author and publisher specifically disclaim all responsibility for any liability or loss, personal or otherwise, that is incurred as a consequence, directly or indirectly, of the use and application of the contents of this book. Before starting a weight-loss plan, a new eating program, or beginning or modifying an exercise program, check with your physician to make sure that the changes are right for you.

ISBN: 1535058269
ISBN-13: 9781535058261

DEDICATION

This book is dedicated to *you*—you reading this right now! May it fill you with positive energy and supercharge your spirit. I also dedicate this book to all the amazing angels who shared their personal stories of overcoming hardship. You never gave up, you never gave in—*and you made the decision to win*! And especially to my loyal and dedicated VIP Fitness friends at www.JNLFitnessStudioOnline.com that I have the sincere pleasure of helping you to transform your lives through powerful principles of personal excellence. I believe in *you*!

TABLE OF CONTENTS

PREFACE BY ANTONELLA CHIARELLA

The current health-care system in the West is successful in combating illnesses and diseases. Everything that does not belong in our bodies is cut or lasered out and eradicated. What cannot be completely eliminated is treated with medication. These problems always seem to be bacteria, elevated blood pressure, depressive thoughts, and so on, and the corresponding medications are antibiotics, antihypertensives, or antidepressants.

In spite of the fact that so much has become feasible, a large portion of our population is uncomfortable with this orientation of medicine. According to a recent survey conducted by some of the most prestigious universities—like Harvard, Yale, and Oxford—when faced with illness, more than 60 percent of the population pursue combined treatments of Western medicine and natural therapies with homeopathy, herbal medicine, Asian and Far Eastern medicine, and some healthy exercise. Among people with previous experience using alternative healing methods, the number who support such a combination of therapies is as high as over 80 percent. It is a clearly observable tendency that people want to combine the best methods of both medical traditions.

What is the basis for this desire for additional support with a different style of health care? Is it the search for natural medicines that support the body in its healing process—like proimmunostimulants, propsychotherapeutic medications, or prometabolic agents instead of *anti*-everything? This desire has also been clearly demonstrated by Western medicine through the application of conventional vitamins and nutritional supplements—despite their not achieving the desired effects on account of being artificial. Or is it due to the emphasis of the alternative medical traditions on interpersonal human care? People feel as if they have been externally controlled by our modern health care and medical system, broken down into component parts, subjected to cold technology, and abandoned. Also, medical interest begins only when sickness is already apparent. Disease prevention and health-promoting lifestyles, however, are issues that are simply neglected. The self-determination of the people and the mind-body-spirit connection fall to the wayside. Western medicine takes action only when our bodies are already sick and only treats the symptoms—not help to prevent them. The causes of some health disorders are also not a major interest for our medical system, so doctors are not addressing the roots of these illnesses.

In contrast, respect for the laws of nature through the preservation of internal equilibrium is at the center of natural health care and alternative medicine. To live in harmony with nature, we live according to the balance of all forces, which adapt and influence one another. Through healthy practices like restorative sleep, appropriate exercise and nutrition, and even benevolent thinking, we decide whether the balance is maintained, and our spirits reflect this balance through a healthy satisfaction, serenity, and inner happiness.

This book about successful life stories should reveal to you the innate and acquired powers in these individuals on the path of healing. You possess these powers too! And you can awaken and maintain them. Whether you have small or large problems, with a holistic perspective, you can strongly influence your body's change and development, helping it stabilize properly and then restore health.

Well, any change in life begins with the first step, and this is by far the most difficult part of it. Therefore, I recommend all who aspire to a successful lifestyle change to seek assistance from those skilled people in the corresponding fields. Without support, the path to becoming healthy may be incomplete, and the individual potential may remain hidden due to doubt and misconception.

I really do encourage all those people who are struggling with a physical or emotional health challenge to open up to the message of the life stories here! They offer you proven paths, facts, and techniques to authentic healing. Drawing upon modern science and also Eastern healing arts, all of this provides a systematic approach to identifying, mobilizing, and releasing the life-damaging beliefs that contribute to addictive behaviors, chronic pain, depression, obesity, chronic fatigue, anorexia, irritable bowel syndrome, and many other emotional and physical health problems. The information in this book will help you understand and come closer to a healing path in your body, mind, and spirit.

My dear readers, I hope that you become excited reading this book, engage your being, train your self-perception, and gain and recapture self-determination.

I would like to take this opportunity to thank Jennifer Nicole Lee and all my mentors, teachers, and all the shakers and makers who have contributed in recent years through their observations and their openness to dialogue so that this world may experience and understand more and more about the truth and the law of mental, emotional and physical balance.

Antonella Chiarella
Shiatsu Instructor & Therapist—certified
Gymnastic Teacher—certified
Shiatsu Mentor & Supervisor

FOREWORD BY ANTONELLA CHIARELLA

Jennifer Nicole Lee is not a fitness model because of her good looks, because she is the best fitness coach I have had up to now, or because of her virtually tireless energy level. JNL is a true fitness model because she can connect to us. She becomes like a best friend or family member. People book her fitness classes because they feel that Jennifer is pleased with their success. She gives the feeling that she experiences our change with us, and in the process she touches our hearts. In this manner, she is directly connected to our newly acquired fitness success.

I do not believe that she was aware of how much she would help others when she decided to liberate herself from her own health imbalances. But today, she does help others!

There is a difference between reverence and love, and she calls on love, not reverence as many other fitness coaches do. This is what makes her the premier expert on the fitness scene. She is worth seeing because she is fantastic. She is loving and unpretentious and will meet your expectations.

She laughs at everything and mostly about herself, and that makes her so authentic. When you seriously want to grow in fitness and well-being, JNL is always there for you. And that, my fitness friends, is what really matters in the end. Time and appointments do not matter for this woman.

This book represents the journey that she and many of us have been allowed to undergo and is a testament to what people in the harshest, most desperate, and most insurmountable circumstances still can accomplish. This book will surprise everyone and convince many critics that anyone can achieve good health, strong fitness, and inner harmony.

Whatever the world connects with fitness today, one thing is certain: everyone can be fit!

Good Fitness and Health Are Not an Illusion!

And trust me: if you don't believe this right now, then this book will convince you. JNL and all those who have achieved good fitness and health know it is true because they live and experience it every single day. And we all believe in and fight for you so that you can do it too.

In love and appreciation to Jennifer Nicole Lee, my ultimate fitness and life coach who always believed in me.

Antonella Chiarella
A JNL Fusion Fitness Friend
Shiatsu Therapist, Mentor, and Supervisor—certified
Zurich, Switzerland

CHAPTER ONE

Jennifer Nicole Lee

Hello, and welcome to the *best* time of your life! Yes, that's right. Just by reading this book, you have set yourself up for major success. By reading all of these stories from real people who decided to take control of their lives and become *victors* instead of victims, you too will gain a whole new surge of motivation to *never give up* and *believe* in yourself. I know that we are all very busy women, with homes, families, friends, significant others, and our own personal beings to take care of, so for volume 2, I decided to make a quick and efficient reference guide below called "The Motivational Kick in the Butt Success Principles" that will help you achieve the winning mind-set that you need fast. I also urge you to revisit this book often as it is the best source of instant inspiration that you need to comfort you in times of darkness, shedding much-needed light and love and showing you that, yes, life is not easy, but you can and will get through any and all situations if you just *believe*!

Motivational Kick in the Butt Success Principles
1. Believe and Never Give Up If you were to ask someone what phrases they thought of when my name was mentioned, I know they would say "Believe" and "Never give up." I say these phrases every day to myself and to my beloved clients and fitness friends. They are the foundation of my positive mind-set and grateful spirit. They are the most powerful words ever because you can't achieve something unless you *believe it*, and then you must *never give up*! When I weighed over two hundred pounds after the birth of my children and had a stark, horrible past of yo-yo dieting up and down the scale with no real *long-term* success of achieving my goal weight

and then maintaining it, do you think I believed in myself? That I could actually now, with two little babies, finally lose the weight and then make it stick? I didn't have a choice not to believe. You see, something happens in your spirit after you become a mother. A fierce fire of passion and determination, a fighting spirit, is also born. And from this new power in my spirit, I focused on my transformation. I decided that I was not going to be just a fat, overweight mom who wanted to bounce back after having children, but I wanted to change my identity to that of a well-seasoned athlete and a fitness professional. So I had a lot of work to do, and I knew it wasn't going to be easy, but I did *believe* in myself—because again, *I had no choice!*

I was a mad woman on a mission. I would do whatever it took to finally get a hold on my weight-loss success, come hell or high water. I wanted to be a mom who was focused, on time, of clear mind, always in the know, and full of boundless energy. You see, my mom was always in a cloud of mental confusion, very emotionally unstable, and not very well organized. I saw her suffer in her own self-inflicted confusion and emotional distress. I knew that was not good for me as well, so I had to flip the switch. I had to become extremely organized and focused and make every second count in my very busy day as a mom. So I did believe in myself, in my method, and that I would get my results and have them stick! I told myself, "Jennifer, even if no one believes in you, *you must believe in yourself!* And so what if you failed before so many times in your weight loss! That's not failure; that's only results telling you what didn't work. Now it will work! Just eat healthy and exercise and give yourself the gift of time, and it will happen!" So I took a bold leap of faith and started my weight-loss program, taking it one day at a time.

Three months passed, and the scale didn't budge, and my clothes were still tight. I got down and a little depressed. I said to myself, "I'm doing all of this work, scheduling in my workouts, being very focused in my eating-clean plan, and still *no results?*" And then I asked myself, "Is it worth it?"

And then God came into my head and said, "Yes! It is still worth it as you are exercising and getting fresh blood and oxygen to every cell in your body, and also you are eating so healthy! Those are the benefits to rejoice in, even if you are not at your goal weight yet. You have more energy for your children, and you are happier and healthier—*so don't give up!*"

I listened to God and kept at it. *Then it happened!* It was as if the *flood gates of fat* opened up, and I started to see the results that I had always dreamed of! My fat melted off to reveal strong, sleek, athletic muscle tone! My prayers were being answered. You see, God wanted me to learn that even if I didn't see the results, it wasn't about the external appearance or the number on the scale. He was training me to *never give up and to believe*! And to live a healthy lifestyle for deeper purposes, like to become a focused, hands-on, positive mom full of energy, with get-up-and-go! Not just to eat healthy and exercise to have superficial results like "looking hot in a bikini." So as you can see, I had to learn the hard way to have my weight-loss stick and not just last a few months, and this journey has been so worth it! So, from one woman to another, *believe and never give up!*

2. Dream Big One very powerful and fun mental exercise I do daily is to *dream big!* I love the excitement of using my imagination to envision what I yearn to accomplish! It's true that if you can see it in your mind, you can hold it in your hands! Just like this book! The contributing authors whose stories will empower you and liberate you all knew that one day they would be published authors! And now it's happening! You see, thoughts become things. *So dream big!* Have fun with this exercise. Do it with yourself as an exercise to see your future as bright, fun, and happy as you want it. See your dream body, dream home, dream job, dream vacation, dream bank account, and dream life in full. Know that if you can see it in your mind again, you can manifest it. It takes the same amount of energy to think small as it does to think big, so go ahead and *dream big!* And just be careful what you wish for as your thoughts are so powerful that they will become true!

3. Why Not You? I love the principle of *why not you?* This is going to really give you a motivational kick in the butt! If you stay on the sidelines of life just watching everyone else have fun, do what they want, and achieve their dreams and goals, well, *why not you?* I want you on the playing field of life, making the big winning plays, moving toward the right direction! If anyone deserves to *create* and *manifest* their goals and dreams, it is *you!* I urge you to put yourself back on your to-do list and set aside at least fifteen minutes per day to focus on your dreams and goals. First of all, we must know what our dreams and goals are. So get clear on what you want to achieve in the next six months or by your next birthday, and then in one year, two years, three years, four years, and five years. Make a list of your short-term goals and long-term goals. Make a plan of action to work toward achieving your short-term and long-term goals. Remember, goals are so important! Life without goals is like a boat without a rudder; it just goes all over the place and burns out fast! So take it slow and steady, and have a laser-like focus on taking the right steps every day to making your goals turn from thoughts into reality! And most importantly, *make it fun!*

Ask yourself these questions: What is holding me back from going after what I want out of life? How can I get rid of these blocks? Do I really feel that I deserve this?

You have got to get real with yourself, and then go for it! Remember, there is no one more hardworking, dedicated, focused, and deserving of your dreams coming true than *you!*

4. If Not Now, When? We are all waiting for the "perfect time" to take action toward achieving our goals. But as a certified life coach, I'm here to tell you that *the right time is now!* And that there will *never, ever be a right time* in the future. The right time is just an illusion and a "baby blanket" term of comfort for the lazy ones who put things off and never take action. You see, while everyone is asking whether the glass is half-full (an optimist) or half-empty (a pessimist), I'm here to say, "I don't care how much liquid is in that glass, *you better just drink it now before someone else does!*" Now that's the winning attitude of a positive opportunist! *Go for it now!* When you see an opportunity, *grab it!* Or if there is no opportunity, *create one!* When you see the most successful people in the world, *they created their own opportunities!* Most of the time their shining moments are all *staged* and created in advance. So going back to the other note, *why not you?* Stop wasting time and *do it now!* Time is the biggest illusion of all. It goes *so fast!* Father Time waits on *no one!* So you can either be an enemy to time and waste it, or you can be on time's side and be effective and efficient, create your winning master plan, and take action ever day toward your goals. So let's start *now!*

In closing, I went to a seminar a while back. An elderly woman stood up and cried tears of sorrow. She said, "All you young women, don't let time fool you. I thought I had all the time in the world to achieve my dreams. But I'm here as a broken women who never took the positive action needed to fulfill my dreams and goals. So I beg you, please, no matter who it upsets, no matter what your current situation is, no matter who or what is holding you back, *go and feed your spirit!* Go and claim what is yours now before you get old, brittle, and weak like me." I'll never forget that moment. So, not as a gentle reminder but instead with a swift motivational kick in the butt, I'm here to tell you that *today is the first day of the rest of your life!* New goals, new intentions, and new results for the *new you!*

5. Be Your Own Best Friend, Not Your Worst Enemy Banish all negative self-talk. It's that simple. Just stop it, and cut it all out. Replace all negative self-talk with positive affirmations that support you on your mission in life to be better, be more fit, and accomplish your dreams and goals. I remember I would allow that negative inner voice to creep up inside my mind and tell me very bad things about myself. But I finally got control over my mind and became my own best friend. You see, a best friend is loving, kind, forgiving and understanding and also wants to see you succeed. This is the relationship that you must have with yourself. Many of you have children or pets that you love. Now ask yourself this: Would you allow yourself to speak nasty, hurtful things to your children or beloved pets? *No!* Never! So why do you allow yourself to sometimes beat yourself down. All that negative self-talk does is kill your spirit. We want to do the opposite! Tell yourself beautiful things that boost your spirit and make you feel loved, special, and supported. Replace "I'm fat" with "I may not be at my goal weight, but I'm on my way, one day at a time!" Replace "I'm a lazy slob" with "I will find new fun ways to boost my energy so I can do all the things I need to do with class, style, grace, and a smile on my face!" Replace "I'm ugly" with "I love my unique, gorgeous shape; my smile lights up a room; and God made me perfect!" Positive affirmations are so powerful! So when you hear that nagging negative voice sneaking inside your head, *smash it hard* with a *positive affirmation!*

6. Too Blessed to Be Stressed This is a huge motivational kick-in-the-butt point. Many of us suffer from depression or anxiety. And here is a fun and fast mental trick to zap any stress, depression, or anxiety fast! When you feel any negative cloud moving over your head, go into your *attitude of gratitude* fast! You see, it's like a law of metaphysics that it is *outright impossible* to be depressed or suffer from anxiety or worry when you are listing off all the positive blessings you are grateful for! Banish that dark cloud of sadness quick by listing off all your blessings. Here are some of my all-time favorites that I say daily:

> Thank you, God, for my strong, healthy mind and body.
> Thank you for this beautiful day!
> Thank you for the roof over my head and the food on my table.
> Thank you for me being so blessed while others are facing horrible, real tragedy like death, terminal illnesses, financial disaster, or losing a loved one.
> Thank you, God, for giving me the eyes to see my blessings and to see the lesson in this situation I'm going through now.

So remember, no matter what, you are truly too blessed to be stressed!

7. Put Yourself on a Diet, Free of BS! You got that one nagging friend who just won't stop texting you with drama? How about that one family member who always drags you into a situation that you don't have the time to even deal with. So today you have the authority to put yourself on a *diet*, free of BS! Yes! You heard me right! I love these diets because you have made a decision to not allow yourself to be subject to the poisons of other people's dramas. We only have a limited amount of time in the day to take care of our families, ourselves, and our everyday matters. So I beg you, we must outsmart these situations that are energy zappers and these people who just drain us! A simple solution is to block them from your cell phone or just limit the time that you interact with them.

TRUE STORY: I had one "friend" who just drained all my energy. She texted me all the time and always said things that were like a trigger evoking negative responses. During this time of my "friendship," I felt so toxic! I even started drinking more alcohol as her vibration was so strong that it subconsciously made me do unhealthy things. And get this: when I tried to go work out, *I had no energy*! So I knew I had to take serious action. I made the decision that my peace of mind, my well-being, and my health were way more important than me entertaining her negative rants! After I blocked her and our friendship dissolved, I was at peace! I had more energy, and I stopped my unhealthy habits. I restored my BS-Free Diet! And I'm here to tell you that it's OK to dial back on the time and energy you put into your own blood family also as this too can end up being toxic and bad. Don't get me wrong; *I love my mom*! However, I had to learn the hard way that I'm so much better off with limited interaction with her. We are like oil and vinegar: sometimes we can make a beautiful salad dressing, *and other times we just don't mix well*! My point is that we now have boundaries of respect and understanding, and when I smell some BS brewing up in some trigger remarks she might say, I suddenly "get very busy" and "have to go" as "something came up" because I know what will happen at the end of that conversation if I entertain the BS. It will drain me and zap my good-feeling vibes. So, in closing, dust off your BS radar, and when the smell is popping up, run the other way! And enjoy your BS-Free Diet.

8. Run from Energy Vampires I know you agree with me: In life, you have people who you are naturally drawn to, who actually boost your energy, who make you feel great and excited about life, and who you *love* being around. I call these types of people angels! And then, on the other hand, you have people who drain the life right out of you! You feel them looking at you with evil eyes or judging you or sneering at you, pouring their negative energy your way. I call these people energy vampires. I often joke that these people actually suck the blood right out of you and leave invisible fang marks on your neck! So recharge your sixth sense, get your BS radar out, and make sure you profile all the people, old and new, who are around you. Do they pump you up with positivity or drag you down with negativity? And a simple rule for dealing with energy vampires: *run!* You can't win trying to fight with them or argue with them, so just run the other way! With energy vampires, losing is winning because wasting energy on them is just not worth it.

9. Believe in Angels, and They Will Appear Angles do exist. They are real people who have a message to give you. They also boost your confidence and are the wind beneath your wings. They are very rare, so when you find an angel, do whatever you can to keep them close to you in your VIP inner circle. They are loving, kind, noncontrolling, open, forgiving, and understanding and will open up doors of new opportunity for you!

10. Pick Your Battles "Losing is the new winning." This is my new quote! Think about it: we only have a limited amount of time in the day, and if one of your family members or coworkers just feels the need to pick a fight, just say, "You are right," and walk away. It totally works! They will be like *What, you are not going to stand there and fight with me? What am I going to do now?* They are kind of lost and confused, and you, you're *off the hook* and onto the next! In situations like this, I know deep down that I am right, and I'm not going to waste my precious time, energy, breath, or oxygen on this petty situation. Don't get me wrong; I'm a spicy, feisty Italian woman who loves a good debate and to fight and stand up for what I believe in. But at the same time, I have learned to let my ego go and to be at peace with not having to *prove* I am right. Even in situations where I know that I am right, if I see that a situation is going sour, I just let my husband or kids "be right" for the sake of ending the negativity. And after thirty minutes, well, we all forget about what we were fighting over anyway. So learn to pick your battles; let it go, and let it flow! Save your energy for things that really matter.

11. Be at Peace with Your Solitude The wiser I got in life, the more I realized that I absolutely love my quiet downtime. I used to feel like many others out there that I needed a lot of people around me all the time to feel significant, valued, important, seen, and heard. But actually the opposite happened. Many times after big conferences I would feel empty and sad. I realized it was because just too many people were pulling me in too many different directions for their own personal gains, pleasure, or objectives. When I represented multimillion-dollar supplement companies, the pressure to always promote their products was very stressful on me. Now, since I dialed back and got real with who I am, and what I want to represent in the wellness industry, my solitude has grown. So I urge you to never allow the feeling of having to be everything to everyone haunt you. Stick to your own true purpose in life, and you will enjoy a new sense of inner peace and solitude.

12. Self-Love and Self-Respect The two most important pillars of internal strength are self-love and self-respect. If you don't have these, you will fall, crumble, and allow others to walk right over you. They are your foundation! Just like how a home needs a strong block of concrete for it to stand the test of time, the same goes for you! You must have strong internal architecture so you just don't break when life doesn't go your way or people treat you unjustly. How do you practice self-love and self-respect? By always putting yourself on your to-do list and making yourself a top priority. Long ago are the days when women just had babies and then disappeared into a blur of becoming an "asexual" baby-diaper changer or baby holder and feeder. Moms and women are so much more! And you deserve to always treat yourself as you should be treated. How can another person love and respect you if you don't love and respect yourself? And let's be clear: You don't show self-love and self-respect by always bragging about how great you are or by all the selfies you take and post. But rather, self-respect and self-love are an art form of behavior. A woman who respects and loves herself will eat healthy, exercise, meditate, pray, and enjoy quiet downtime, allowing herself to reflect and enjoy her inner peace. And you don't need to be a millionaire to do this! I also suggest you create a peaceful retreat in your own home, a sanctuary where you can decompress and relax from the busy day. Set up your bathroom to be more of a spa experience by making small investments in some relaxing bath salts, aromatherapy, face masks, and body scrubs. These little weekly beauty rituals tell everyone else that you matter, you take care of yourself, and you respect and love yourself. Or pack your healthy meals when you go to work. Choose fresh fruits and vegetables. Set up your own private at-home training area where you can work out and celebrate mindful movement and embrace your fitness lifestyle. And always say positive things that evoke positive responses. When you take this lead, others will follow and also treat you with love and respect, and your life will transform from just living into a beautiful journey of self-respect and self-love that trickles over and touches others to do the same.

13. Don't Create Hell for Yourself I always say, "Don't create hell for yourself, as other people will already do this for you." It's true! Why create hell and inner civil war for yourself? There is no point. If you want to work out, do it. Don't second-guess it, and don't try to get out of it. And if you want to feel pretty, take the time to fix your hair into a classy fuss-free style, and put on a dab of makeup. Just do it! I had one friend who said she was going to do some-thing, but then she got in her own darn way and never did it! It was like a do-si-do! She took two steps forward only to take two steps back—ending up in the same place and wasting a lot of energy. So when you make a decision, set yourself up for success so you will stick with it, and make it happen. If you want to work out, put out your workout clothes the night before so you are more prepared in the morning. And plan your weekly workouts into your calendar.

They are important business meetings that you can't be late to, or call in sick to, with the most important person in the world—*you*! In closing, create clarity, not confusion, in your own world. Be very aggressive in sticking to your game plan so you won't create an endless cycle of ups and downs and all-arounds for yourself, or what I call a *living hell*!

14. Have Strong Decision-Making Muscles In order to achieve true success, you must develop strong decision-making muscles. There are people in life who are very indecisive, and if they do make a decision, they never stick with it. So I highly recommend that you build strong decision-making muscles. In life, we are forced to make decisions every day. Sometimes people take forever to make up their minds because they are fearful of the outcome. As a certified life coach, I'm here to tell you that you will be in certain situations where you have to make a decision where neither of the outcomes is favorable. But you still must make a decision and, more importantly, *stick with it*! When you make your decision, it is always important to be *confident* about it! Have the backbone and the "balls" to make up your mind. Be confident, stick with it, and never look back. This is one of the best tips I can give to anyone reading this book. It will save you a ton of time, and others will see you as a real leader.

15. Flush the Negativity I know I have many Motivational Kick in the Butt Success Principles, but this one has to be one of my absolute *top favorites*! When we use the bathroom, we flush the toilet and move on and out as fast as we can, right? Well, what about in life? When a bad situation turns up or something horrible happens or somebody says something we don't like, *we just need to flush it* and move on. You see, I know that there are things we can control, and we must focus our efforts on these. But with the things we can't control or fix, we must flush them and let them go into the huge "commode of the universe." I have to be honest with you: I'm constantly flushing negative energy and situations all day long. Sometimes I just wake up and keep that handle locked down in place, so just as soon as the BS shows up, it disappears just as fast! *Swoosh!* So if a bad memory is haunting you or you can't get over a horrible event in your life or you are suffering from being "crucified" or wrongly "skewered" by someone out to get you, *you have to just flush it* and *flush it fast*, or this negative energy will infect all the positive areas of your life and being with its toxic dirtiness!

16. You Get What You Focus On Your mind is an extremely powerful tool connected to the universe. No, this isn't some hokey-pokey hippie talk; it's real. Google it, and do the research. You will find that the world's most intelligent metaphysicians can actually prove that your mind creates more of what you focus on and makes it into reality. My weight-loss success story is a direct result of this. I had a "before" photo that I placed next to an "after" photo of a fitness-magazine cover model whom I wanted to look like. And not only did I achieve my weight-loss goals and transform my body, but I went on to also be on ninety magazine covers. And the same thing goes for my home. I envisioned my house before it was ever built. And after two long years of looking for a home, my husband and I decided to purchase a one-acre lot and build our home. When I sat down with the architect, he had a sketch already designed for this lot, and it was the exact same home that I had in my mind!

The same mental process goes into how I met my husband. I was in Miami for a good year and had a horrible time dating. Then I prayed, "Dear God, I'm ready to meet my soul mate, and not only that, but my future husband and father of my children." That night I went out, and I met my husband. You see, what you envision in your mind's eye, or third eye, and what you focus on, you will create and manifest into your life. Again, sometimes it happens fast and sometimes slow—but it does happen!

In closing, I want to remind all of you that, again, we only have so much time in each day. So choose to focus on the solution, not the problem. Life is not perfect, so instead of focusing on how bad things are, focus on what you and your close loved ones can do to make it better or solve the problem.

17. What You Speak about You Bring About The power of the mouth! The power of your words! I'm extremely careful with what I say and what I acknowledge in my conversations, quietly with myself and out loud with others. You see, the universe not only hears what you are thinking but, more importantly, hears what you say out loud. Be extremely selective with how you talk and what you say because you are actually prophesying. If you say today is going to be a horrible day, it will be, because you already declared it a bad day, and bad things will happen and show up. But on the other hand, if you say, "I'm so excited for this day as I will accomplish so much, and mercy and favor shine upon me," you better just get ready for the good times to roll! So choose to speak words of love, happiness, joy, abundance, faith, celebration, and success! And at the beginning of each day, say out loud, "Today is going to be an amazing day filled with miracles and huge success breakthroughs." And at night close out your day by saying, "Tonight I will enjoy a peaceful sleep full of rest and relaxation, allowing me to jump out of bed in the morning full of energy and pep in my step." Just try it! The power of the spoken word is more powerful than we know.

18. The Power of Visualization As goofy as it sounds, vision boards work! So make a wise but inexpensive investment in a cork board where you can pin your favorite photos of your dream life. You see, you can create your life just the way you want it: with the perfect mate, home, car, body, health, and financial security. Your vision board is a powerful tool to daily remind you why you are working so hard and why you are so focused and driven to succeed. So rip out pages from a magazine of what you want to be like or have. And have fun with this exercise! As your dreams and goals change, so will your vision board. It's like a menu of the universe, allowing you to select what you want and what you are willing to work toward and focus on. Place your vision board in a sacred, private place in your home where it will be free of unwanted ridicule or criticism. Remember, this is *your* vision board, and you have the right to dream big and envision your dream life. Also, at night when your eyes are closed, visualize your dream life. This is also a very strong mental exercise. NASA has astronauts visualize their walks on the moon. So if mental visualization exercises are highly emphasized in NASA astronaut training, I know it will work for everyone!

19. Hard Work Pays Off You can have all the skill in the world, but if you are allergic to working hard, just forget about it. You see, hard work will always trump skill or talent. There are a lot of talented people out there, but they are not willing to work hard. I love hard work because it gives me the best returns. If I work hard, I always get results, and I always get one more huge step closer to achieving my goals. So fall in love with hard work, and never shy away from it.

20. Be a Positive Opportunist In order to win at life and to achieve your goals, you must become a positive opportunist. As I said earlier, while the pessimist is so busy telling everyone that the glass is half-empty and the optimist is telling everyone, "No, the glass is half-full," the positive opportunist is drinking the water and enjoying every sip, not even concerned about how much water is in the glass! They are just like, *I better drink this before someone else does or before it dries up!* So always be positive, and when you see an opportunity, *go for it!*

21. Paralysis by Overanalysis Some people get "stuck in stupid" because they are too busy overanalyzing. They overthink too many things and never take action. I had one client say, "Well, JNL, if I lose weight, I'm gonna get saggy skin, and I don't want sagging skin." She was thinking way too much, and it totally confused her, held her back, and paralyzed her from taking action. I was actually kind of secretly embarrassed by her thinking process and said to myself, "Would she rather die of a heart attack or become really paralyzed from a stroke and still be overweight because she didn't want saggy skin?" I was shocked by this.

In another instance, when we know we need to take drastic action in our lives, our own minds come up with long lists of things that block us and again force us into overanalyzing the situation,

14

paralyzing us. To outsmart this, we must do what I call "chunking it down." We must see our goal and then chunk down the action steps. We don't want to overwhelm ourselves, which again just freezes us up. Never overanalyze the situation. Take it one step and one day at a time. And enjoy the journey.

22. How and Why I Created my JNL Fusion Workout Method

This is not a sales pitch. I truly want you all to know how and why I created my JNL Fusion workout method. I created this method out of my own frustrations I had as a busy mom, not having enough time to train but needing max results in minimum time. I studied all the top training methods, took the best from each, and fused them all together. I also wanted a workout that fused together the mind, body, and spirit, filled with positive affirmations that help me get through tough workouts and keep me wanting more! I also knew that my body was not burning fat when I only did my weight training. So I weaved thirty-second cardio bursts into my traditional strength training. I also knew that I didn't have the luxury of spending two hours working out, so I made each session no longer than forty-five minutes start to finish, including warm-up and cooldown. I wanted a method that fed my spirit, while challenging my body, and that I could do in the comfort and convenience of my own home, a method that would help me to lose fat while toning up muscle, give me energy, build up my endurance, and fuel my stamina. And there you have it, JNL Fusion! This method literally saved my life. I was overweight, sad, depressed, and going nowhere fast. I was falling into the trap of my mom and her mom and her mom—the long lineage of all the women who just gave birth to their children and became invisible baby caretakers. I wasn't happy. I was always exhausted. Had no drive. No vision. No focus. So I decided I was sick and tired of being sick and tired. I envisioned the dream women I wanted to be: focused, confident, kind, and full of positive energy, the kind of woman who lifted up people's spirits and whom people wanted to be around, not run from! This workout method helped me achieve becoming who I wanted to be—fit, fun, and fabulous! I also hope this workout method helps you to achieve your weight-loss and muscle-sculpting goals in a fast, fun, and efficient way, allowing you to have more time with your family and loved ones and more time on your personal projects and goals. In closing, I had to stop the *confusion*, so I created the *Fusion*! I pray it has helped to heal you and make you happy and whole from the inside out!

23. Fitness Is a Journey, Not a One-Time Event As your coach and fitness trainer, I'm here to remind you that fitness is not just a one-time event but, rather, a journey—a journey to be enjoyed! You don't go to church once and become spiritual the rest of your life! Just like how you don't take a bath once and then are clean the rest of your life. The same goes with working out. You can't train once and expect to be fit your entire life. So make fitness and working out part of who you are, part of your spirit, and part of your weekly rituals. Aim at working out no less than three times per week and no more than six. You should aim at getting to your goal weight and then maintaining it. I'm here to tell you from my own personal experience that I did it, and you can too! I lost over eighty pounds after the birth of my children in 2003, and now fourteen years later, I have kept it off and only gotten stronger. And listen to this: If you fall off your program, don't stress! Just get back up and get back on. In the past fourteen years, I have experienced times in my life when it was hard to squeeze in a workout or I made bad food choices. But the *one thing* that kept me going was my decision to *get back on track*!

I like to use this analogy: An airplane is 99 percent off-track going from one city to the next. But its autopilot keeps checking the compass and adjusting its direction. It gets there and lands safe and sound. The same thing with you: always keep your eye on the prize, and adjust your fitness lifestyle program to get to your goals!

Final Closing Notes to My Angels I pray that my Motivational Kick in the Butt Success Principles have opened your eyes tremendously; touched your spirit; and helped you to become more successful, happy, and confident! Please e-mail me with your success stories or how this book and our fellow contributing authors' stories have helped to heal you and show you that all things are possible.

As I now open the book to the following chapters of motivational stories, please know that I love and appreciate you. Thank you for allowing me and the highlighted authors to motivate and inspire you to be better than you were yesterday! And I do believe in angels. And I thank you for being an angel in my life! Cheers to your future! Your success is my success! I believe in *you*!

xo JNL

CHAPTER TWO

Antonella Chiarella

Undefeated
Life Balance Mastery by True Guidance

Welcome, my dearest readers.

I am very pleased to share with you in this precious second book of motivational self-empowerment how to achieve sustained life-balance mastery by receiving true and loving guidance. The wide benefits and deeply affecting consequences of a well-balanced life are and have always been so fundamental for human growth and well-being that they should be taught in every school, culture, and social class today.

Times are changing toward progress in public health-care education, and with our book, we want to ride on this wave to support the positive effort coming from all directions in this field. Therefore, we have made it our mission to share all our experiences and newly acquired knowledge in life balance with the world.

Maybe some of you now think that this is just another book of success stories.

Well, my dear readers, this is a book of real and sustained life-balance-mastery stories, which are based on all the most natural and healthy methods and packed with a lot of authentic, strong self-belief!

Long before science believed and researched in it, not to mention talked about it, all our authors here practiced the traditional truths of finding healing resources for their life balance. With this book, we're showing you the evidence that mastering balance is way more possible than many people dare to think. So with us the all-natural way of life is back for good!

I'm sure everybody has heard by now that there are no quick fixes for building up and keeping a healthy lifestyle. Well, we tell you here that there are and always will be *natural* fixes! We're all living proof that taking a holistic approach to achieve sustained health and life balance is possible.

So, self-empowerment and life guidance for achieving significant changes and mastering your balance in these confusing times have been given a voice. And the heroes here are all just like you and me!

My dear readers, we wish that after having read all our unique stories, you might also recognize yourself as a fighter and self-believer because all evidence from the field of psychology shows that everybody either is or should sooner or later be his own master of balance. This self-mastery lies in the nature of life itself! Therefore, we encourage everyone to look deep inside himself and find that quality to fight and overcome every obstacle that life throws at him.

My Way to Real Life Balance
A Tribute to True Guidance

Thanks to the silent but so impassioned and devoted help of deeply caring people around me on my journey to survive all the overwhelming ups and downs in my life, today I can practice as a fulfilled and well-balanced therapist. Against all obstacles in my early childhood and adult life, today I truly can live a happy and fascinating life. I went from intimidated and abandoned to undefeated and outspoken, an independent woman in every sense.

I developed the skills of complementary therapy in acupressure based on traditional Chinese medicine and Eastern healing arts. Before that, I started my career in gymnastic therapy.

Everything began with my initial university studies in pedagogy that drew me toward approaches in identifying, mobilizing, and releasing the life-stagnation beliefs that contribute to many physical and emotional problems.

Simultaneously I nourished a profound interest in bringing attention to *two central topics* in developing and mastering a sustained life balance:

The first of these topics is how the benefits of natural cures and the power of our nature's healing influences are available to and affordable for any human being. Through to the wisdom of traditional natural medicine and the latest breakthroughs in neuroscience, psychology, and modern medicine, I experienced the fact that the body-mind perspective has to be released from core beliefs and painful memories that contribute to emotional stress and physical illness. The core message is to free all these factors step-by-step to heal and move beyond the restricting conditions that have been limiting our health and happiness.

The other topic is how you cannot succeed in mastering life balance without true and loving guidance and care from the right people in your family, like friends in a supportive society. Here and now, my coauthors and I dedicate ourselves to truly and firmly practice public guidance. To reveal the deep underlying truths of overcoming life's biggest problems is the duty of our times, and we want to show how fundamental it is for a person seeking help to recognize and accept the best guidance they can find.

It is very dear to our hearts to discuss this truth. Achieving inner peace and personal freedom is a basic step toward realizing your dreams and visions in life. And we have dedicated ourselves to helping those in poor circumstances who might have given up hope. They deserve to know all about the hidden truth, because that's the real and authentic truth. All our authors have been there and hit rock bottom very hard, so no one knows these challenges better than them, and you deserve to hear the raw facts and how to become a fighter from real people who have done it themselves!

We want to share with you the newest scientific evidence and news about the large amount of natural possibilities that life offers to everyone. And our core message is that finding balance is not achievable for only the privileged and professionals, celebrities, or important personalities. In fact, we want to open up and join the dialogue with them because, especially today, it is all about finding true balance and, most of all, true wisdom! And we can learn only from professionals in this field who truly and honestly walk the walk and not just talk about it.

The vital importance of human guidance and mentorship is therefore becoming a reality more than ever. We all need psychological and emotional support and unconditional love to have a chance at becoming strong and, most of all, developing some healthy, well-balanced personalities. So we all owe the highest respect to those human beings who actively live strong moral and ethical lives behind the scenes—who take action as helpers and givers and guides and become significant mentors and leaders. These kinds of people are around in all levels of society. They really make our world go around and help bring balance to it! They do not hesitate to stand up for their deep human duties that come right from their hearts, no matter when or where in the world. With this book we want to show what makes self-believers and their helpers necessary role models and, in the end, our heroes.

Mastering My Life Balance

My personal balance was thrown upside down through experiencing the fracture of cultural systems and boundaries in the deep south of Italy in the '60s. During those times in South Italy, there was still a strong patriarchic and Roman Catholic–oriented culture on the one hand and a very loving family culture with a deep sense of brotherhood and a big heart for children on the other. Women and the young generation had to strictly follow that strong religious orientation, as well as abide by male-dominated family structures and a sealed South Italian social life. Divorcing at those times was seen as an ethical betrayal, and women filing for divorce were condemned and sometimes isolated from society. In other words, seeking a divorce was social suicide in those times!

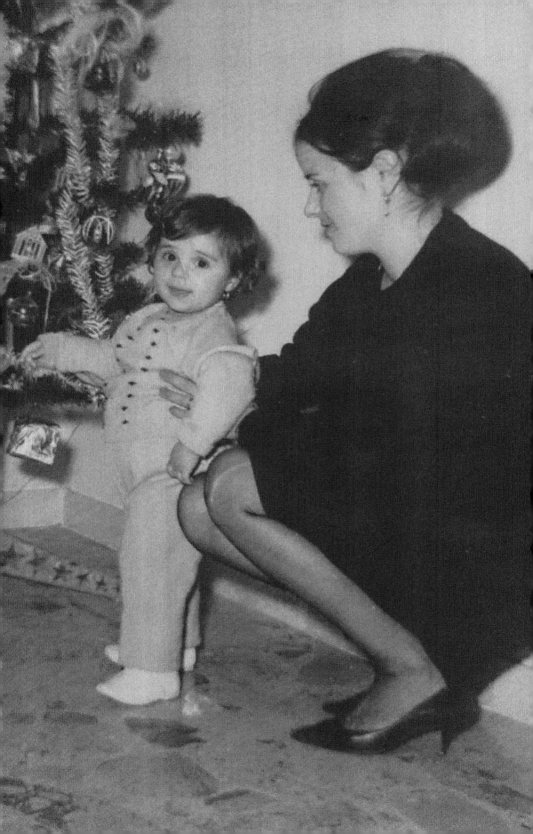

Absolutely nobody saw it coming in my family, but at a young age, my mother unfortunately had to seek personal freedom to achieve the best life balance in raising me as her only child. That charming and loving husband who my father had been before the marriage suddenly turned into a strong loyal son of his very South Italian family clan. To my mom's and my bad luck, this meant that married life fell into the classic rigidness of Italian tradition.

After long struggles and tough fights caused by that suppressive cultural structure from my father's side of the family, one day my mother finally found the courage to file for divorce, and with that our painful social suicide was about to begin! The war in the family with endless battles for child custody raged like there was no tomorrow and continued with no end in sight. It was devastating and traumatic for me, and the shock affected everyone deeply. And against all taboos, my mother's family stood up for her the best they could. But my mom, after trying really hard to fix her marriage, had to end it. My father lost his temper and started to organize an undercover breakup behind my mother's back. The tragedy was completed when my dad took the unfortunate but classic emotional divorce action of child kidnapping. Desperation and hate led his heart at that point. He even organized a child hostage master plan - I was kept from him as a hostage for almost 1 year behind locked doors and hidden keys, which threw me in the deepest shock! I could not leave the house in any sense! And a devastating, never-ending divorce trial started.

My dad used his strong personality to win all the battles he wanted to fight, and in this one he was particularly adamant. So I was separated from my mom and the rest of her family, and all of that happened in the name of love, family loyalty, and God. Well, my future balance and life stability just ended right there.

My dad made accusations, started a mobbing and conspiracy action/mode against my mother, and played scary games to intimidate my mother in front of the family, friends, neighbors, and mainly in front of the court system. In those times the men's world stuck together to save one another's honor, and my father's case was no different. My mother became a victim of the corrupted court system of the '60s in the South. Nevertheless, despite her youth and financial struggles, she put on her strongest iron-lady demeanor with the toughest poker face she had, confronting the whole situation in court all by herself. She did not hold back and filed a second divorce round without the help of any lawyer at all! In the very end, surprisingly for everybody, from my dad's family all the way to the mayor of the city, the game finished badly for my dad. And before the game was over, the judge had to give in to my mother's determination to declare war on anybody who wanted to take away her only child! She made her perspective loud and clear that if they wanted to have a war they could have one. Strong, big, and loud like the good old Italian style! Unfortunately, the evil game went on with the judge's most severe decision. He gave both my parents child custody but ruled that I take a side at only the age of five! So I was given only one week to make up my mind on the most important decision of my life, which would determine my own future and way of life. With that sword in the neck, everybody's nerves were as tight as guitar strings!

At home during that horror-scenario phase of the trial, I got wrapped into another princess bribery treatment, but kept as a hostage at my grandmother's house! A family clan mission in the biggest South Italian style started fast and furious. My grandmother came into full action! My dad was her only son. He was the man in the house and her prince son, so, as his firstborn child, I was the princess of his clan!

For that cuddling bribery treatment, my grandmother took out her biggest mother-in-law secret weapon, which was nothing other than the famous Italian cooking skills. Day in and day out, she started early in the morning turning her kitchen into an "Italian best food service," always with a smile and the brightest sparkling Italian eyes. She did not leave out one of my all-time favorite childhood dishes. Well, it really was all paradise that week, but I was not easy to turn around. And believe me, great Italian food always worked out well with me! But that time it was all about to talk me out of a life with my mom and force me to forget all about my loving aunts, uncles, and sweet and loving cousins on the other side. So making me drop my love for my mom's family from my heart did not work out at all! Therefore, my grandmother pulled out her tried-and-true Italian matriarch way of playing grandma! She played the family clan drums loud and clear and made sure that everybody in the family showed up at the house day in and day out—for their clan duties and everything that could turn a little princess's mind in their favor. From spreading lots of sweet love around with lots of sweet chocolate, to giving me big hugs and long cuddling sessions with long playing times. But meanwhile, my parents' divorce trial got into the final round. That was the end of the beautiful Italian family life that we could have had for the rest of our lives. Instead, it all ended with a heartbreaking divorce and family war. Nothing was left out in our family soap opera!

Well, all that was very heavy on my shoulders. And because of that long hostage time, I had already made up my mind. At my father's, things were very traditional, and at my mom's, they were very free-spirited, so I knew that by making one wrong step, I would end up going straight into my daddy and grandmother's family's kitchen hell. With the divorce fight, I had completely lost my childhood balance and the balance for my future at the age of five. My harmonious family future flew right out the window. My parents completely severed contact, and for more than twenty years, I had no communication with anybody on my father's side. Hate and anger remained behind and caused irreconcilable differences between my parents and their families. I loved my dad very much, and I felt he truly loved me the same way back as his first child. My dad always won his battles, as he almost did this one, but this time he and all of us lost everything that was worth fighting for! Our family life with a strong balance, everything was gone for good! It showed to everyone that in the end, nobody had won anything, but everybody had lost everything by losing the most precious thing: the precious love and bond between all of us.

Well, as I told the judge my decision to live with my mother, inner peace was not even close to us. My dad was hurt and speechless about my decision and absolutely determined to get me back by any means! So the chase went on again for years to come. My dad was very much torn apart by his love for me on one hand and by his family's pressure and social critics on the other hand. Now, slowly but surely, his social suicide had begun! The fact that his young ex-wife could win over him was nagging at his pride. So a desperate underground battle of getting his child back started all over again and went on for years. After having understood my dad's and his clan's next intentions, my mother made a drastic decision to save the situation and keep my father far away for good. In a last-minute self-reflection, she left her parents' home and emigrated with me abroad on the late-night international train.

For me everything was falling apart, and my heart was broken deeply. I realized that we had to create a second home. We came into a foreign country with a foreign culture and a damn complicated foreign language…Swiss German was certainly not like Italian! And Italy and Switzerland were like day and night! But we had to leave behind everyone and everything, especially our pride. I was home-sick like crazy! No grandfather, no cousins and aunts and uncles, and mostly no grandfather were there anymore.

At this point, my young mom had to build up a home and future from scratch. She started with nothing and just one job, and she took on two more jobs later. She tried everything possible to build up a new existence. Meanwhile, the distance was not enough for my dad, and he still tried behind the scenes, through his friends and colleagues, to stay informed and proactive for making his next move.

From that time on, my everyday life turned into hell. It was a constant struggle for survival. It felt as if we were still in a battle and staying ready every moment for the next attack. I developed post-traumatic behaviors from the fear. I had a strong sleeping disorder and suffered from nightmares for a long time, but I could not tell anyone. I was scared to death that my dad could show up again in disguise and take me away for good this time. I was not told that he was not allowed to cross the Swiss border without being arrested. But my mom could also not put one foot back in our country to reunite with our family because she had made her desperate move to go abroad. My dad had child custody there too. And for years we could not even dream about going on a holiday trip back home to

Italy! We were just the two of us, alone. As emigrants without any family there, we felt as if we were living in nobody's land, and I just felt completely lost and isolated.

My mom was not there to help me with all my inner demons. She worked day in and day out and even during the night. Going to preschool was like hell for me. There was absolutely nobody protecting me from my dad possibly showing up. Only as I caught the eye of my kindergarten teacher did I experience a joyful and stable time for one year in her class, and I have kept that period deep in my mind ever since. She understood my situation and gave me supermom VIP protection treatment with her highest attention during class! She let me live at her house for three weeks. And those three weeks made me grow like a little sunflower! She was the love of my life! And she is still to this today!

Later on at school, we emigrants were regularly under threats of violence from other kids who always tried to beat us up. The little girls, but especially me, because they knew I was alone at home. We were just the dark-eyed spaghetti eaters and meatball fanatics from the South. But I didn't even like the damn meat sauce and greasy meatballs! They kept telling me horrible stories of horrible crimes too. I was intimidated constantly. Soaked with sweat and out of breath, I always had to rush home. Every single day my way home was like walking on long and horrible hot coals. I hated to go to school, and at this point, I hated the whole world and mostly my family. They were not around to help. I was desperate not knowing how to put an end to this damn scenario! It felt like drowning and being in an earthquake at the same time. This went on for years, and my desperation grew so high that I filled up that internal pain by not staying home alone anymore under any circumstances. I developed a sense of detachment from my family and tried desperately to cover up that emptiness and sadness. For all these reasons, I started taking classes in theater and gymnastics, playing basketball, and staying at my friend's house for days. I tried to overcome my lethargic life with being the best in my hobbies. That affected my life so much because it was about so much more than just working to get good grades. I was searching for a way to feel safe and free and trying to find my place in this life outside my family situation! I finally wanted to have a real purpose and a safe structure for my life! But that would have to happen way later. Shortly after I discovered watching TV. And this new habit helped me to keep dreaming and moving on from my daily inner demons. With watching movies, I also had finally found some role models.

The family situation at home ruined my entire ability to study well and to have a bit of confidence and enough energy for making good grades at school. I had no life balance at all as the constant flee-ing and hiding took my breath away. I was all alone at home because I had no siblings, and my mom was working like nuts to pay for my piano lessons and a good education. She took action and took life by the horns, and late at night she started to learn how to write on the typewriter and eventually took the chance to leave the heavy work in fabrics and changed to office work. There she was finally with office colleagues and not surrounded by construction workers any-more. She also found a calm, interesting, and intelligent life partner, which finally changed our lives for the better.

The first years at school I could not stick with the math classes. I just could not talk in front of the class because I was so insecure, and I was tremendously terrified of all kinds of exams. I loved foreign languages, and I was one of the best at them, as well as in handcrafts and art. I loved to be creative; it calmed my spirit. In sports I could not keep up the energy at all. I was a disaster in climbing mountains, jog-ging, or climbing the monkey bars All in all, it really was a horror for me. I was always with the one who came in last. My best girlfriend was very athletic and into gymnastics and tried to cheer me on, but I was always last. Nevertheless, I kept my enthusiasm for sports, and Nadia Comaneci and Magic Johnson were my heroes. Soon I found my big love for music and dancing, and I tried them all. I stuck through doing it just for a sweet distraction from home's reality.

Well, but for math and science classes, I was put under a lot of pressure, and I was constantly wishing I could find someone who could help me out of my grades mess. One day I finally got to know my nice next-door neighbor, who became my daily babysitter and our family friend. She wasn't blessed with children, and I became her little friend from next door. Growing up near that lady, I got back some confidence, and some things turned out well at school also. But growing up I felt that I had to be successful and not fail at life, and I had to leave my dad behind. Those worries made me grow up fast!

In those difficult times, I could only dream of a better economic life, so I started to work hard during my holidays in restaurants as a dishwasher and sometimes in the kitchen to help the cook. I also dreamed about stable and strong relationships with intelligent and great people who believed in me and my dreams. Mostly I wanted a warm and safe home where nobody could touch me! So I wished to leave everything and everyone behind me, and that decision suddenly was not difficult to make anymore because the sad news about my grandfather's death gave my dream of future family reunion the final nail in its coffin. My mother's family, which was the only one I still had, fell apart after his passing. There were irreconcilable differences in the family, and everybody went their own ways. On that day my world crashed. I felt abandoned all over again, and the hope to get back the bond I had left with all my lovely cousins was gone for good. After years dreaming of a reunion with them, the possibility was gone!

Therefore, after having almost finished school, I had to make the decision again how to restart my own life and to come out of that stifling family circumstance with my dad's constant chase. One day, sick and tired of being the victim of my parents' fight, I made the decision to close out the life with my whole family for good. It was a very hard decision at the time, but I had to just to finally find peace and freedom.

I moved out from home at the age of seventeen and a half. Since then I lost touch with my family and my country for more than twenty years. And I walked my walk all alone again. I stood with nothing on the streets. I had to build up a new home with no balance, no structure, and no help, just with one wish in my head to finally find freedom from my childhood's past and my dad. I wanted to feel free, alive, and happy forever.

Finally, at university, a gentle student gave me all the attention I needed. I leaned on him for better times. I built up a strong bond, and that student became the love of my life. After years we married. Finally, I had my harmony back, and the marriage was one of the happiest and most important times of my life. For the first time in my life, I experienced true and lasting life balance! I was so motivated to go for my dreams that I finally started to fly with my own wings. That man on my side was a teacher himself, so I gave everything I could to make everything work.

But over time I was not able to live my visions anymore. The reason was that my husband did not believe in me and my dreams anymore! It became so hard to move on with my life when I realized that he was not developing the same visions and meaning of life that I was. Conflict after conflict followed. Over and over again, he wanted to convince me that his way of life was best, but it was just not mine. And he told me so many times that I would never become a professional. He called me a fantasist and illusionist. In the end I had to file for my own divorce. I was devastated, and my whole world again fell apart, especially seeing as how the man whom I loved and trusted so much had tried to push me over the edge! And years of difficult breakup matters with him followed until I was free again.

I found my way out of the darkness by standing up for my rights. It cost me all the energy I had to start a new life all over again. While I was curing my wounds from this battle, I knew this time I had to find the guts to move on all alone for a certain time because I was not willing to live with someone else! At a young age without a single penny in my pocket, no family around, and not yet finished at university, I had to walk my walk once again alone. I felt as though my heart had been ripped out of my chest and that I could never feel safe again. Because of all that, I became very lethargic again, and I tried just to move on by surviving day by day. Nobody ever believed in me, so I had to believe in myself!

I came out of that dark space only by holding on to my dreams and visions. And this time my life taught me one big lesson: that I had to live not just a simple dream but the biggest one I had in my veins! And for that I needed someone for help. One day at a meeting, I met a really gentle and humble therapist. He became my very best resource for life guidance. And with his help I started to study my favorite subjects all over again, which were rhythmics and gymnastic therapy. I started moving again, and finally I got my rhythm back. I understood that it is all about the balance in life. And of course, it is all about unconditional love and true life guidance to find balance! And with that wisdom, I finally could bond again with my family and cousins! Today we meet in the summer for long holidays, and sometimes our hot Italian tempers come through very hot again. But we would not break up and lose our family bond again for anything in the world!

Today, as I am myself a therapist and mentor and because I have gone through my journey of mastering balance, I can confirm that lack of love and guidance affects our life balance on all levels of being. Lack of love manifests in many disguises. It may appear in autoimmune disorder, allergies, anxiety, and panic attacks. It can emerge through obesity or anorexia, depression or low self-esteem. Even digestive problems, chronic pain, and fatigue can all reflect underlying emotional malnourishment. Dealing with challenges to your emotional and physical health can be exhausting, but if you are willing to look at the story behind your illness, release the toxic emotions you've been carrying, and begin thinking and doing things differently, healing and transformation will happen.

Some Last Good Advice

I have experienced that our ability to give and receive guidance and love influences every aspect of our lives, including our health. The best advice I can give is to look for good and real friends who can offer strong life guidance and steer you with unconditional love and respect! Only someone with that ability can show you how to identify and release the core beliefs and painful memories that contribute to emotional distress and physical illness—freeing you to heal and move beyond the restricting conditions that have been limiting your health and happiness.

My dear readers, today, after having survived all the breakdowns that turbulent family circumstances can bring, I have some good advice I think everybody can use.

I have created my own rules for mastering a strong life balance, and today I am having the best time of my life and living on my own terms!

Don't be afraid to walk your walk alone, if necessary.
When you want to fly high, sometimes it's lonely up there!

Love heals—fear kills!

Empower yourself—stand up for yourself.

Always believe in yourself, even if nobody else does!

Stay true to yourself, and always be yourself.

When you need help, hire a mentor.

Always believe in yourself, even if your mentor doesn't!

Build up your base,
and surround yourself with the best.

Play your cards right!

You are not your condition; move on and your dreams come true.

Learn the rules to break them.

Have a dance!
Keep your body moving; it lights up your spirit.

Enjoy your life!
"…every day is a party!
And with the joy of life you can conquer the world!"
A Latino's wisdom.

CHAPTER THREE

Susan Losier

A Helping Hand

My story begins on a warm, sunny day on July 14, 2008. All was well with my life, or so I thought. Just two days prior, my then-husband, our six-year-old son, and I went out for supper with my son's godparents for their anniversary. We had a great time, but that night my then-husband said he needed to get something before the stores closed…he never came back that night or the next. My son kept asking, "Where's Dad?"

Two days later my then then-husband came home and said, "I don't love you anymore."

I wasn't really shocked as deep down I *knew* there was someone else. I asked him, "How old is she?"

He said, "Sixteen," as though it was no big deal.

I thought, *What the heck? That's sick!* He was forty-one years old, and she was a schoolgirl of sixteen! I looked straight at him and told him, "*Get out!*"

He left, and my son came downstairs asking, "Where did Daddy go?" Heartsore, I told him we were going to his godparents' for a visit. My friends were awesome and said we could stay with them however long we needed.

Since my then-husband's girlfriend lived in the same neighborhood as my friends, it wasn't long before we saw them together. I found out a short time later that she wasn't sixteen at all but fifteen!

Now I know what you're thinking, *Ewww, gross!* That's exactly what I thought! Needless to say, I was a mess, and things went from bad to worse real fast!

I told my then-husband not to take her to "our" house until I could get my things from it. I was feeling overwhelmed and numb at all that was happening, and my health, which isn't the best to begin with, worsened. The house and property were large, and with all my health issues, it was too much for me to take care of by myself. At this point my then-husband came up with a really great idea for the both of us! He asked me to let him and his girlfriend live in the basement apartment so he could be closer to our son!

My brain did some mental calisthenics, let me tell you. I mean really! Of course, I said no!

When I went back to the house to get some of my and my son's things, I was not really surprised to find that he had changed the locks so I couldn't get in. With him it had always been about controlling the situation and the impression of what others saw. My warning bells went off immediately as I knew he was hiding something he didn't want me to see. His girlfriend had been wearing some of my clothes and jewelry, so I suspected she had been in the house and going through my things!

So I did what I had to do: I broke the window in the basement and entered my house. When I went upstairs to my bedroom, what do I find? Her clothes were there, intimate and otherwise! Furious about his breaking our agreement, I quickly threw some things together and went back to my friends' place.

As I mentioned earlier, I have health issues—colitis and asthma among other things. Now, as you may or may not know, with colitis you are going to the bathroom, *a lot*! By this time it was totally out of control. Anything I ate would go right through me, and I began losing weight fast, getting weaker and tired beyond belief. I was losing a lot of muscle tone, and my hair was falling out, enough to make me nervous.

During this whole period of time, there were constant demanding and abusive texts and phone calls, as well as having my then-husband constantly drive by my friends' home just to try to intimidate us. It didn't take me long to figure out he was deliberately doing this to cause my illnesses to get out of control. He was well aware that stress and other things triggered flare-ups as he had had to take me to the hospital at various times during our marriage.

The time had come to a get lawyer as he was wanting things all his way or no way. The police suggested that because my then-husband was stalking us in various stores when we would go shopping or following us with his truck all over town, we should seek a restraining order. I didn't have a car—and still don't—so I had to rely on my friends to get me to doctor appointments, take me shopping, and so on. So, following the advice of several officers, my friend and I both tried to get a restraining order so that we would have at least the semblance of some kind of safety and less stress when trying to go about a normal routine in town.

After two full days of testimony with several witnesses corroborating his stalking of us, our request for restraining orders was denied. You can imagine our disappointment. Knowing how my then-husband thought, I knew him feeling he had won would only embolden him to continue and even escalate his behavior. Which proved to be the case.

Not long after this, when my friend, her son, and his wife were on the way home from shopping, my then-husband tried to intimidate her by attempting to run her off the road with his truck. We had court the next day, and this was his way of warning and scaring us into dropping things as he said he didn't want to deal with the courts and lawyers.

She was so scared she was shaking and crying and trying to keep it together for me, and I was trying to keep it together for her, which was hard for both of us. However, none of us were backing down! We called the police again, but after they took my friend's statement at the police station and an officer went to the Crown, they said they didn't have enough to go on.

I was now coming to find that I was fighting not only for my rights and my son's against my husband, but I seemed to be in the position of having to fight a flawed legal system as well, both of which I felt ill equipped to do. Not knowing where to turn, my friend's husband got on the phone and found the number for the woman's transition house in our area. He talked with a woman and told her my story. She immediately said that she wanted to meet us, which we did. It was the best thing I did, and I feel during the last seven years she and her coworker have not only been allies and advocates but friends as well!

They would tell me stories of other women and what they were going through, and it helped me know I wasn't alone. Due to being depressed, sick, and having to take the time to deal with so many different agencies, I just didn't have any more physical and mental strength to give, and I stopped working out. I have always been a creature of habit, and before my life fell apart, I had a routine of working out in my home with all my exercise equipment. Since I had left my home, I felt displaced, and with my equipment still there, I didn't have the strength, drive, or incentive to push myself to even try to continue in my workout routine that I had developed over the years.

I have always been a fit person; some might say even fanatically so. I became a fitness instructor back in 1994 and was a personal trainer. I found this very fulfilling in my life, and I loved it!

Three months after my then-husband and I separated, I finally got my own place close to where my friends were living for their continued support. I was beginning to try to pick up the pieces of my life and live independently, but I was scared as I hadn't been alone for nineteen years. I barely had any furniture, as most of it was still at my old house. I was blessed to have friends give me some of the basics, for which I was very grateful, but it also somehow made me feel like a failure!

Friends were telling me that my then-husband was telling people, "She'll never make it on her own!" In essence, he was then reconfirming what I was already feeling about myself. He was hoping and wishing for me to fail being on my own. To prove that I needed *him* to somehow make my life a success.

I am now proud to say that, far from pulling me down and making me want to give up on my life and my son's, it triggered a response deep within me I was unaware I had. A deep inner chord that made me dig my heels in and say, "Oh yes, I will!"

So, after some deep breaths, determined inner talk, and support from my friends, I was able to go back to my old home and get my exercise equipment, weights, step, and other fitness equipment and tapes, even with my then-husband looming over me. I have to confess that I was still scared and shaky inside, and I know I couldn't have done it without my friends being there for moral support, as well as helping out with their vehicle. My then-husband had always had to take control of the situation, and he insisted on loading my weight-training station onto the truck. It was a good one, big and beautiful—and, oh, how I loved seeing my old friend again! I could feel a tiny sprig of excitement begin to grow as I thought about getting back into my routine, getting back into shape, and getting my health on track.

When I got back home, I happily began to put it together. However, my joy quickly turned to depression when I saw that several parts were missing. My then-husband had kept the bolts to it, and I couldn't put it together. I wanted to cry! My friends and I tried to find ones like them, but I couldn't find any. So there it sat in my living room, my once-beautiful "friend" standing there useless. It seemed to vividly reflect what I felt my life had become: useless, broken, and not worth anything! I too had vital pieces of myself missing that had held me together, and looking at that piece of metal only reinforced all that I felt I had now become, and I was heartbroken and defeated. I threw it out. There were so many times in the last several years that I just wanted to give up and give in, but my friends never let me. They were in my corner every step of the way with such encouraging words when I would feel I didn't have it in me to keep on breathing, let alone fighting. They would say things like, "You are worth it," "You are stronger than you know," "That's what he wants you to do (or think)…don't let him!" Their love and caring for my son and me I will never forget.

At this point I will just say my friend's name. Verna knew I was a fitness nut, and to try to motivate me, she would ask me to go for a walk with her. We lived right next to the ocean, so to go for a walk was just what I needed. We—my son and Verna and I—would all put on our sneakers and head out the door! It was a real effort on my part, but seeing my son's excitement and his smile brought a smile to my own face and rekindled that deep determination in my soul that I had almost forgotten. It gave me that mental boost I needed and missed, and I think that's where I started to truly realize that working out gave me the mental clarity I needed.

All of us began daily walks, especially after supper, and greatly benefited from getting out in the fresh, invigorating air. It gave us a much-needed, healthy break from the hectic chaos that we were all going through, from doctor and lawyer appointments, court, therapists, and so on.

Another positive turning point in my life—of which there have now been many, I am happy to say—was when I was shopping at Walmart with Verna and my son. I was getting him a movie in the electronics section when I saw a CD with a beautiful woman on the cover that said, "Fabulously Fit Moms by Jennifer Nicole Lee."

The title appealed to me as a mom, and her shape brought back pleasant memories of when I too was fit. So I picked it up, read the cover, and put it in my cart, not realizing at the time the changes that little CD would bring to my life both inside and out!

After we got home, before doing anything else, I ripped off the plastic, popped it in the DVD player, and did the workout. Wow! I fell in love with it right away! It somehow stimulated my brain processes in a more positive and enlightening way as dormant receptors became alive again. Over time, my self-esteem began to climb as the endorphins began to flow once again.

Through my exercise routines that I began to do regularly and therapy discussions, I came to see my life in a new and positive way. I began to realize whenever my then-husband would text me, drive by my house, or follow us in the car, I would begin to slip back into a negative pattern of thinking. However, now I had found the *key* to change that pattern, and I was going to *use* it to lock the door against negativity and unlock the door to a bright new and healthy life!

I began doing breathing exercises recommended to me by my therapist, and she encouraged me to keep working out, which I did. She also showed me how to take my power back and how to *keep* it!

One thing I haven't mentioned yet is that amid all the turmoil of what my life had become was the disclosure that my son made to a babysitter. He said that his father had been "touching him" in a way that made him feel icky! Well, when I heard that, I went over the top! Now, not only was I dealing with severe health issues; a child-cheating, manipulative, and controlling then-husband; but also the knowledge that my son had been being abused by his father! My stress and frustration rose to new heights!

One would think that a child's safety would be of utmost importance to the agencies that are in place to help protect them. All I can say is that from my personal experience, the courts just don't seem to get it, and it's very frustrating and unfair to children! I came to realize real fast I had to be my son's voice and that he needed me more now than ever.

I had to be strong for him, and it wasn't just an option but a necessity. I needed not just to be healthy and fit physically but also mentally. I remembered the saying of Susan Powter, who I still love, when she said, "What is the most dangerous animal on the planet…a pissed off mother," and boy was I now pissed off! (Don't ya just love Susan Powter?)

Fast-forwarding two or three years after my son disclosed and all the difficulties that came with that, I was following Jennifer Nicole Lee on YouTube. Oh, and did I mention I didn't have a computer either? My friends have let me use theirs for the last few years. I love them so much! I watched her workouts and followed them as best I could. I picked up her *Fitness Model Diet* book and read it cover to cover and started to follow her workout routines. Things that I had learned years before in my course as an instructor came rushing back to me, and I was working out again!

I was getting really fast at bringing up her workouts on the computer anytime my then-husband texted me or drove by and I felt myself getting worked up. It was as if she were right with me in the room, and I would just do a quick workout to help bring my equilibrium back in balance. It kept me grounded and released any anger or other negative emotions that were building up inside me. Afterward, I would feel so good and strong that I wanted to keep that feeling inside of me all the time. That is why I kept on working out and continue to keep working out even now! I never miss my workouts, and I am a better, stronger, and happier person for it, and my son and friends began to notice the positive changes that were happening in me, which only emphasized to me the benefits that come from taking care of yourself inside and out.

I knew I was beginning to do better physically, but mentally I still had a way to go. I began to do yoga again and immediately felt the soothing and restorative results. I was looking through Jennifer's videos and came across one where she was talking to some women about her book *Body Mind and Soul Diet* book, and I thought, *That's it!*

I ordered it, and when it came in, I started reading it right away. I discovered another key to unlock another door that I had been overlooking. My head had been disconnected from my body.

I knew that in order to be there for my son for what *he* was going through, I needed to be well mentally and emotionally *myself*. My friends were there to keep me motivated to "never give up," to the point where I can now motivate myself much more easily! I began to learn it was OK to take quality time for me and that, in doing so, it didn't mean I was selfish or a bad mother or person for putting myself first. In fact, it was just the opposite! The stronger I became mentally and emotionally, the better equipped I was to handle and cope with all the emotional needs my son had. That is another lesson I am proud to have learned, and I am continuing to grow and learn new things every day and then seek to find ways to pass on my insights to other mothers who may be going through similar things as I have for the sake of their children.

Another thing I haven't mentioned was what my son's disclosure about what his father did to him triggered inside of me. It unleashed a horde of demons from my own childhood that I had buried years ago. Demons that I had wanted to keep buried in the past to be able to cope with the now. However, memories of what had happened to me as child, long held behind a dam, began flooding back. This is where my therapist really helped me. She was awesome! She saw me shut down and cry, and she always said that I was in a safe place and heard my story. She was a family doctor first and then branched out to psychotherapy. She wanted to help people on a different personal level, and she has done that for me. Encouraging me to speak about my past and present and to help me live for the future. She let me see that I'm a fixer: I try to fix everyone, and my friend Verna is the same. Isn't that what we as women instinctively want to do—help others?

Another big thing that helped keep me going was, of course, my son. There were many times when I just wanted to give up and say, "Forget it. I'm done." But then my son would come into my room and give me a big smile and hug, and my heart would flip-flop, and I knew that I had to find the strength to keep on fighting for him. I knew he was suffering every bit as much as I was. Every time he would see his father, he'd immediately go into a rage! He couldn't eat or sleep for a couple of days afterward. He couldn't sit still or concentrate on doing his schoolwork. I have home-schooled him since he was five, except for a year when his father forced him to go to public school, which didn't work out very well for anyone. He also started to see my therapist and another therapist, and they determined that he suffered from PTSD directly connected to what his father had done to him and what he was continuing to do. I needed to be there for him emotionally, as I was still going to court practically every month and meeting with lawyers every month. I found it very difficult, some days more than others, to pretend things were OK and going to work out for the best, especially when I would come back from court trying to hide bad news or decisions from him to keep "his world" as safe and secure as I could.

Living, coping, and dealing with all the things that have happened in my and my son's life to this point have proven to be a life-changing and continual journey of learning and discovery.

Discovering that even when I was at my lowest point in my life with no home, no money, and no idea what I was going to do, I was not alone, that there was a bright spot—friends who offered their home and hearts with wide-open arms, giving my son and me a safe haven to begin rebuilding our lives again. Coming to realize that I was living in a toxic relationship and the best thing for my healing was that I had to go through a *detoxing regime*, and that sometimes we have to go through really bad things in the healing process to get the best results.

I learned how to detox not just from food but from people as well. Leaving my toxic religion caused me to lose most of my family, and I must say, there were many times when my then-husband was harassing my son, my friends, and me that I felt so alone. I missed calling my mum and hearing her voice say, "Everything will be OK."

I also learned that in hard times you find out who your real friends are. The ones who stick with you through thick and thin, and that there is no shame to go to them and ask for help.

I discovered that there are a lot of people out there who do care and want to do what they can to help. Two such blessed women were at the transition house. Through their experience and time, they helped me with various appointments and pointed me in the right direction of resources that were available to my son and me. They went with me to court and sat tirelessly for long days, sitting on hard benches just so that I wouldn't be alone. They drove me to appointments when my friends' car wasn't available. They were really great, and I can never thank them enough for all the selfless work they did for my son and me and other women as well! A lot of women in this line of work have their own sad stories that generally lead them to helping other women in transition, and their support is and should be appreciated by all.

So where am I now?

Seven years and seven judges later, I am proud to have won a judgment of sole custody of my son with no access from his father, and it was the best day I had had in years!

On June 10 of this year, my divorce went through! I am ecstatic to be able to say I no longer have a then-husband but now have a *no-husband*! I am finally *free* and ready to spread my wings and fly! With help and inner strength, I kept my faith and never, ever gave up!

My son is more content and getting happier by the day now that he too feels free and safer. He still deals with PTSD but is learning to control it better. His uncontrollable rages and sleepless nights have lessened greatly since the divorce. Our children rely on us much more than we know. Since time immemorial, women the world over have been and will continue to be the nurturers, healers, teachers, and protectors to our children. If we are not well physically and emotionally, our families suffer, and this has been borne home to me through my trials and healing that we women are much stronger than we know!

I hope telling my story does at least one thing...

I hope that it lets you know you can do whatever you put your mind to—that you are not weak or helpless, even though you might feel like it, and that you are not alone nor without hope! You are not being selfish to take time out for yourself, whether it is for a fitness workout, meditation, calming baths, needed naps, or an energizing walk. You deserve that time; heck, you need that time.

I guess you could say I "found myself again" after many years. Was I lost? I feel I was; I was lost in my own life.

Motivation for me was in the *doing*. It was making that determination to pick myself up off the floor and restart and reshape my life. To find my booster cables and give myself a much-needed charge. If I begin to hear those old soul-destroying messages that weighed me down, I now stop and drown them out with thoughts of how far I have come and where I want to go and how I am going to get there!

So, when you hear that nasty little voice telling you you're not worth it or that you should just give up, shut that voice up! Kick it to the curb and say, "No more! You're not welcome here anymore. Move out and move on!" You can do it; believe me!

As women this is how we can help one another: through our stories, which speak about our fears, hopes, and accomplishments. We can hold one another up, pat one another on the back, and say, "Well done!"

Don't look back at that old life; there's nothing there for us anymore. We need to keep looking forward and begin writing a new story and building a future for ourselves that will bring a positive way of thinking and being that will open us up to a bright new life!

I now have a wonderful home; some money (not a lot, but some); and my wonderful friends Verna and Blaine, who have stood by my son and me even when my *ex* (how sweet the sound) gave them so much trouble. They are still beside me, and it is times like this that you find out who your friends really are.

I work out five times a week with Jennifer on her www. JNLFitnessStudioOnline.com website. I love the routines because I can get a great workout in a short time, and I always feel great after, as if I can take on the world!

Remember motivation is in the *doing*!

So, get doing!

Every journey starts with that first crucial and tentative step, as I know all too well, and your first step could be opening this book and reading the living stories found within *our* stories...

You won't be taking your step(s) alone! We are here with you in spirit and practice. I will be honest and tell you it won't always be easy, but you can do it! Women throughout the world will always be here for you, and Jennifer will always be there for you.

I remember someone telling me that when you can tell your story without crying, you are truly on your way to being healed. As I am writing this and remembering what my son, my friends, and I have been through, I have cried a bit, but it is getting easier. Even now doing yoga, I still cry, but that is part of the detoxing and healing, and I feel cleaner and lighter afterward. So don't be ashamed if you do cry; we are supposed to as it's part of being human. And one day you and I will not be crying tears of sadness, pain, or regret but tears of joy and hope as new chapters open in our lives.

So if you are reading this and my story has helped you even a little bit, you have made my heart happy. Please don't be afraid to ask for help, or if someone gives you their hand, *take it*! We all need a helping hand at one time or another, and when you accept that hand and experience the support along the road of healing, life becomes easier, and then you will grow your wings and fly! I wish you all the health and happiness you richly deserve. Be well!

Susan B. Losier

CHAPTER FOUR

The Dynamic Duo

To Hell and Back

*W*arning: Before you read this, we want you to understand that we are doing this to show you that we are not perfect in any way, shape, or form. We have been down, we have faced more than one tragedy, we have faced adversity, but most importantly we have fought back and seen the light. We hope that you take something away from this, and we would love to hear any feedback or hear your story.

To Hell
We want you to read this paragraph; then we want you to close your eyes and picture this being you.

Four o'clock in the morning, three days before Christmas, you're eighteen years old, you're a senior in high school, and everything in your life is going so well that life couldn't be better. A priest and a police officer knock on your door, you run into your older brothers' and parents' rooms to see if they're all there…Your father is not there.

Your heart sinks to the floor, and you ask, "Where's my dad?"

The priest and police officer sit us and our family down and tell us that our father has been killed in a car accident.

We can't process it, we can't breathe, we are cold and have chills running down our spines, and our vision is blurry…the only thing we can hear is our mother screaming and crying, "Nooooooo!"

Our life has just been turned upside down as fast as you can snap your finger. We hoped and prayed it was just a bad dream and we would wake up soon.

We begin to realize that our eighteen years of happiness just got crushed, and for what reason? A reason nobody will ever know. That so-called light of happiness just got a dark cloud over it, and we realize our family will never be the same again.

We entered hell at the age of eighteen and knew we had a long road ahead of us to get back. We had the picture-perfect life, and now it had all been taken from us.

We knew that our ultimate provider, our leader, our role model to mold us into men, our father, wasn't there to guide us in life anymore.

Growing up we lived a very structured life with school, sports, church, and family time. Our father was a correctional officer at San Quentin State Prison before he passed away, so you can imagine he was pretty strict and made sure we had daily structure. He once told us, "Nothing in life will ever be given to you. You have to work for everything you want, and if it's too easy, then find something bigger that challenges you." Everything he had taught us up to that point would have to be practiced in the real world on our own. Trial and error as society likes to call it.

Our father had a relentless mind-set; he was the ultimate provider for our family and one hell of a role model to us. We get our personality and wild side from our mom, which is a great balance. We watched our father's work ethic each and every day, and that rubbed off on us. When he passed away, we had our dark times, but we found a way out because we were relentless as well. We knew we were always in the fight and to never, ever quit, and we prevailed after many years of battling.

After his death, we made a promise to ourselves that we would be there by our mother's side for however long it took us to graduate college.

We would sacrifice going away to college, we would sacrifice getting the college experience by living on campus, we would sacrifice being able to take spring breaks to exotic destinations like normal college students do, and we would work to help pay tuition and bills at home.

This wasn't the way it was supposed to go down for us. But we swallowed the curveball, that tragedy that had occurred, and we manned up and did what we had to do to get through it. We developed a relentless mind-set and form of mental toughness that we never knew we had inside of us.

Six Years of Being Lost

From the age of eighteen to twenty-four, it was all black roses and darkness. We were lost, we were angry, we were frustrated, we were mad at the world, and we wanted to inflict pain on others because of what we were going through, and we did not know any better.

We got into fights when we would go out. Our mother became an alcoholic even though she never used to drink. She also became addicted to antidepressant pills. We lost a piece of her when our father went, and it was one of the most difficult things to witness and adapt to. It broke our hearts seeing our mom in such pain. Our older brother was lost as well and dealing with his sorrow differently from us. As you can see, we had no one to turn to and no outlet.

We were distant from our family members, holidays would never be the same, we were on academic probation, we drank three to four nights out of the week, we had been arrested several times, and we had spent the night in jail a couple of times. All things our father would have been so disappointed with.

Our closest grandmother (our mom's mother) passed away three months after our father did due to cancer. Another ton of bricks hit us when we couldn't even grasp the thought of our father being gone. Our mother was nonexistent, and we had no clue how to help her. All we could do was be there for her. We had no guidance, no direction, no mentors; we had enemies, and at the end of the day, all we had was each other.

The Light

At twenty-five we started to see the light at the end of the tunnel. There came this point where we stopped feeling sorry for ourselves and realized that the only way out of hell was to get ourselves out; nobody was going to feel sorry for us. We ended up graduating and earning our degrees that year, we invested in a property with our close friend in our hometown, things at home were starting to get better, and everything ahead was starting to look positive.

At the end of summer, we kept our promise and left home. It was very hard to leave our mother and brother, but we knew that it was time to be on our own and live our lives, and she needed to be on her own to reflect on her past mistakes and grow as a person. Living at home was eating us up.

One of the toughest challenges for us through those dark years was to watch our mother, whom we loved so much, constantly drink and use antidepressant pills to heal her wounds. Our mother is the best mom in our eyes, even today, regardless of whether she's the same person who she was before the tragedy. We are very proud of her and would never judge her.

And Back

At twenty-five, we saw this guy's column in a *Muscular Development* magazine at a store, and we were so intrigued by his training and nutrition philosophies that we contacted him and hired him as our coach.

This was one of the best decisions we have ever made in our lives thus far. What he has taught us apart from training and nutrition has been absolutely priceless, and there's no way we could ever pay him back for it.

The values we have learned, the mental toughness, the outwork attitude, the never giving up, the list could go on. It was almost as if our father had sent us an angel to look over us and get us out of hell.

Everything we had been through when we were in hell for six years: all the adversity we faced, all the bad decisions we made, all the pain we inflicted on others, all the pain we dealt with, waking up to a mother who had lost her husband of over thirty years, all the darkness, all the negativity—Dr. Layne Norton basically gave us a key to unlock our true potential.

It was as if it was meant to be to work with this man and be mentored by him; it was a sign of guidance. The combination of his knowledge and philosophies on life intertwined with our six years in hell and brought us to where we are at now, made us the men who we are. It's made us toughen up, look life straight in the eyes, and take what is ours. We have never, ever looked back since, and we will never take our feet off the gas pedal. There's no stopping from here on out!

We were finally through hell and back. We overcame adversity, even though it was tough and we had made so many mistakes along the way; we never threw in the towel or asked for anyone's pity. We just dealt with it to the best of our abilities and learned from our mistakes.

From then on we started Dynamic Duo Training, we got good day jobs, we had our first apartment, our relationship with our mother and brother was good, we took advantage of modeling opportunities, we traveled, we met incredible people in the fitness industry, we invested in mentors, we got certified in training and nutrition, we took advantage of numerous opportunities that arose, and we were finally taking what was ours.

Another mentor we have to wholeheartedly thank is the one and only Jennifer Nicole Lee! This amazing woman took a chance with us and selected us as the winners of her Fitness Modeling Factory West Coast contest. It was such an amazing experience meeting JNL, doing photo shoots, and just laughing at goofy things. What really stood out to us about JNL was how she was so authentic and down-to-earth. We just knew she was a good person and meant well, and those are the kind of people we want in our lives. Words could never describe our gratitude for JNL and all she has done for us.

Till this day we stay hungry for more because the best of the best desire to be on top and stay on top. You can never become complacent as entrepreneurs; you have to outwork your competition each and every day.

Wrapping Our Story Up

We just want to make it crystal clear that we didn't write this to have you feel sorry for us or to brag about our accomplishments.

We wrote this because we don't want people to think that we are perfect and that our journey in life has been all sunlight and roses. We have had many rainy days and will continue to going forward. We know others around the world are dealing with worse tragedies, and we hope our story and fight to get out of hell can inspire others.

We want to be authentic with our clients, friends, community, supporters, and most importantly ourselves. We want to share our ups and downs with all of you because we know many of you out there have experienced tragedy.

We want to live a life worth telling a story about so we can inspire, educate, and motivate others.

Everyone deals with adversity, some more than others, but at the end of the day, you still have that choice to live your life to the fullest and reach for the stars, and we all control our own destinies.

You just have to want it more than others and be willing to overcome the sucker punches that life throws at you and understand that you can never quit because you are always in the fight!

If we went to hell and back, so can you. What's your story?

Thank You

CHAPTER FIVE

Tracey Jared

Stroke of Luck

Life was good as I turned forty-six in 2011. A couple of weeks after my birthday, I woke up and went to work as usual, feeling no different than any other day, but this day would change my life forever. I was a secretary in a small office in Illinois, where I grew up. For a couple of years, I had worked at the local YMCA as a fitness instructor in which exercise was a big part of my life. I was talking on the phone to a customer, and he said to me, "Ma'am, you sound tired." I continued talking to him and could hear my words slurring, and my left arm just dropped off the desk. Then I had tremendous right-eye pain. I thought, *I'm having a stroke.* (I knew about strokes because my dad had had three ministrokes and one major stroke after his open-heart surgery.) I collapsed out of my chair and onto the floor, and I thought I was yelling for my boss, who was in the next room. But a coworker came out front where I was, saw me on the floor, and ran to get the boss. They picked me up, sat me in a chair, and called 911. They could tell I had had a stroke because one side of my face was drooping.

In addition to being a fitness instructor, I also had my own business teaching Zumba five times a week. Going for a walk was also a daily regimen for me. So I was in pretty good shape, which was a good thing because exercise saved me. The massive stroke was caused mainly by uncontrolled diabetes and because I had gotten my neck cracked by a chiropractor a couple of days before my stroke. He cracked my neck with such force that it tore my carotid artery, therefore loosening a clot that contributed to my stroke. The hospital was able to give me an injection called TPA (clot buster), which helped. This clot buster came with some possible complications, though, like brain swelling or bleeding that would require the doctors to operate. So I was put on a life flight to the nearest city that had a neurological hospital. There they did an angiogram on me trying to find where or if there were more clots. My family is so awesome; they all pulled together to be there with me, and my three sons were very brave. I'm sure it wasn't easy to see their mom like this or hear what the doctor had to say about me. My attending doctor told my family he didn't know what the outcome would be and that he was unsure of how much brain damage was done. After this massive stroke, I had to go through rehabilitation. I would soon discover that everyday activities like getting dressed and tying my shoes were very challenging, as if I were in kindergarten again. I first learned to walk using a walker, progressed to a quad cane, and then finally graduated to a single-point cane. Very frustrating to say the least, but I was determined to get better. After all, I had a new grandbaby on the way and already had a grandchild whom I was able to hold, hug, and play with. Exercise and being fit helped me with my recovery. Doing everyday chores like cleaning, doing laundry, and doing dishes was a great way for exercising my hands and furthering my rehabilitation. Exercise had helped me survive a stroke, making it my stroke of luck! A couple of my nieces decided to do a benefit for me because I didn't have insurance but had a lot of medical bills. That benefit was a few months after my stroke, and it was a huge success. My history of exercise also made my recovery much easier than expected. So my age and being fit really helped me recover from the stroke much better than someone older and living a sedentary life would have been able to. I still have some disabilities since coming home. Sometimes I have an issue with my left foot dragging. Plus, I have limited eyesight in both eyes (no left peripheral in both eyes), so I can no longer drive. It is disappointing because I can't work now either. With these issues remaining after I came back home, I wondered what I was supposed to do now. I still went to therapy every week, but at home my fitness instinct took over, and I started doing wall and girl-style pushups—anything to get stronger on my left side. I had dumbbells and an ab ball to use. One day I was looking on YouTube for fitness routines and some kind of inspiration. There I found it. I mean her, Jennifer Nicole Lee; her JNL Fusion workouts were something I could actually do. I did modify some actions, but her motivation and spirit were what I needed to get through my days of solitude because I wasn't working. Sitting at home was difficult to say the least. I couldn't even do my Zumba. I couldn't remember my routines, and my left side wouldn't do the moves I wanted it to do. My diabetes was still uncontrolled.

I found my new job was fitness and trying to get my diabetes controlled. Exercising, eating right, and taking medicine were a full-time job for sure. Even typing on the computer has been a challenge. My left hand doesn't type the way it used to, so I mainly type with one hand. Looking at the screen with my limited eyesight is also difficult. I don't see the whole screen. As a result, I don't use the computer very much. My motivational saying is, "Be strong.... Power on!" I never knew how strong I was until I survived a stroke. I have to be even stronger now as I was diagnosed with CLL/SLL (a type of leukemia). There is no treatment for now because I'm only at stage one. Treatment will start when I am at stage three or four, which could take years. So before I need treatment, I just live my life as usual, devoted to helping people be aware of stroke and diabetes and cancer. I do walks for cardiac issues and stroke, diabetes, and cancer. I may not be able to walk the whole distance, but I push myself as much as I can.

I moved with my fiancé to North Carolina. Moving and unpacking were big, but I pushed through the tasks of unpacking and getting a new home set up for us. Then I found a new diabetic doctor who had me start taking a new drug for diabetes. This drug could help lower blood sugars and could help lose some weight too. So I was glad of both possibilities. After two months on the drug, it caused some side effects, and I had to stop taking it. During this time being bored at home, I decided to find a gym to go to. Get me out of the house a couple of days a week at least. I wanted to lift weights, but my weak side made it difficult to lift heavier weights. I found a trainer who could help me lift weights and get me to that one goal of competing. But unfortunately we had to move after a couple of months of training. So I haven't competed yet, but one day I will. I'm fifty-one now and loving life staying fit!

I have spoken to a diabetes group, though I didn't know public speaking would be something I could do. But again my inner strength came through. Teaching an exercise group at the YMCA and teaching Zumba prepared me for so much more in life. My local town newspaper did an article for Stroke Awareness Month. A friend and nurse at the local hospital told them to contact me because I had a great story of survival. I did a phone interview with them. I am so grateful for surviving a stroke and try to help get the word out to help other people survive. The key is FAST; this word is used as an aid to help detect and enhance responsiveness to stroke victims. F: facial drooping, A: arm weakness, S: speech difficulties, and T: time. If any of these symptoms is showing, time is of the essence. Don't hesitate to call 911.

The power of prayer is powerful too. My home church had a prayer chain going for a while. It was so great knowing they were praying for me! One last thing: I don't take life for granted because you never know what might happen! Live your life to the fullest! One day I was living and loving my life driving, working, and playing with my grandchildren. Then boom, a stroke happened, and I wasn't able to do most of these things we take for granted every day. I no longer think about what I can't do anymore. I want to eventually get certified as a personal trainer. To be this, you must look the part, so lose weight and get toned up. Most of the time people can't tell I have even had a stroke. I still follow JNL on Facebook and love her motivational videos and posts. I want to also compete in a figure competition someday soon. May my story help you to never give up or give in!

Live, Laugh, Love
Be strong…Power on!
Tracey Jared

Contact Information:
e-mail: tljared65@gmail.com
Facebook: tracey.jared@facebook.com

CHAPTER SIX

Heather C. J. Atkins

Awakening Health through Compassionate Nutrition

My aim with sharing our stories is to highlight the health benefits and remarkable healing power of whole plant foods. Or, if
you have already come to this awareness, to encourage you to stand
up for what we all know to be undeniably true—regardless of valid
fears we may have of the negative and defensive reactions potentially
extracted from friends and family. I hope these short stories will be a
reminder for you to always remain receptive, to cultivate your ever-
present intuition, and to understand and accept that giving credence
to God's love will oftentimes shed light on a road less frequently
traveled. Have faith that your unrelenting determination and steady
output of effort will eventually result in great rewards, regardless of
what your respective goals may be.

Society at large has difficulty conceptually grasping that our
human physiological dietary needs can be met wholly through the
consumption of plant foods. But why? For most people today, a
belief in the necessity of meat, dairy, and eggs as critical pillars of sus-
tenance has been rooted firmly in early childhood. This philosophy
overlooks an instinctual ethical responsibility pertaining to animal
welfare that lies dormant deep within each and every human's vis-
ceral conscience. Suppression of this instinct due to early-onset soci-
etal indoctrination has dominated the vast majority, leading many
people to endure negative health implications resulting from this
underlying, habitually ignored dis-ease. I personally belong to a bit
of a minority—being one of few individuals born with parents who

chose to respect my vegetarian preferences. Freedom in this regard has allowed for these aspects of my conscience to rapidly burgeon.

A lifetime of intermittent investigation on my behalf has brought me closer to understanding the inner workings of this dominant, tradition-based mind-set; why we have been conditioned to believe that consumption of animal-derived foods is crucial for optimal wellness; why society has concluded that the perpetual torment of sentient beings is deemed inherently necessary to ensure success as a species; and why people continue to choose a diet that has been irrefutably documented to be more insidious and noxious to their health than even that of cigarette smoking.

From what I can remember, my ethical obligations began at age four when I made the independent decision to boycott SeaWorld. I had been given a brochure advertising the park by my stepfather, who had asked if I would like to make a family trip to the park. The image on the cover depicted a massive marine mammal being ridden by her comparably tiny human trainer. This did not sit well with me, as my level of comprehension did not allow me to understand what this orca was doing in a tank instead of swimming free in the open ocean. I expressed my opinion, and we never made that trip.

By age eight, my then-single mother and I found ourselves homeless on the beaches of our home town, Kona, Hawaii. We had been abandoned by the stepfather I had known since my mother and biological father parted ways when I was nine months old. Penniless, along with a host of other grim circumstances, by no means deemed us poor. My mom and I had befriended a good number of organic farmers on the island, and she worked in exchange for produce, eggs, and goats' milk. At that point, I had chosen to adhere to a vegetarian diet due to my above-mentioned ethical obligations, and thankfully, my biological father soon relocated to our island home to offer a solid roof over my head during our days together.

Soon I found myself wondering, *Is it me? Is my ethical vegetarianism simply a contrivance of oversensitivity?* Needless to say, there were countless people who opposed my belief system, and I came to a place of such perplexity that I eventually did succumb to the idea that I was just an overly emotional animal lover—perhaps all manner of fauna were put on this earth for us to eat. I concluded that my respect for all life forms was merely a passing product of childhood innocence and the consequential naivety thereof produced. Eventually, I chose to intentionally conceal my ethical viewpoint from peers and acquaintances in avoidance of the seemingly constant, inevitable verbal backlash. My moral reasoning for abstaining from animal flesh at mealtimes was simply not holding up in conversation.

As years passed, I continued my vegetarian diet, even experimenting with veganism on and off, but for the most part I kept my ethical views hidden. My mother had completed Hawaii massage licensing requirements, and each summer, she and I would spend three to five months of the year at health retreat centers across Europe. When Mom taught massage and yoga classes, I would spend excessive amounts of free time in the kitchen helping the raw vegan chefs prepare food for the retreat-goers and staff. Spending this time with people who shared my affinity for meat-free cuisine instilled validation within me that perhaps there may be some truth behind the axiom of my intuition.

In my teens, my health began to decline because of a sheer desire to conform to the eating habits of my peers. I was still mostly vegetarian yet would allow myself frequent junk food indulgences; this included fried and highly processed foods, cheese, and shrimp on occasion. These choices clearly were not working for me, as I suffered from chronic respiratory infections, systemic candida, and severe stomach flu that saw me hospitalized annually without fail. I tried experimenting with various diets and cleanses that temporarily masked my symptoms, but the ease and addictive nature of our current SAD (Standard American Diet) had me caught in a vicious cycle of junk food dependency.

In 2003, at the age of nineteen, I met my husband, Darryl, a native New Zealander. Darryl's story of personal tragedy and miraculous resilience opened my eyes to how petty my personal fears and insecurities concerning dietary matters really were. What he had gone through would have ruined any lesser person's life. I had so much to learn from his story...

By age sixteen, Darryl had already achieved multiple moto-cross and supercross championship titles in both New Zealand and Australia. As a young person, he struggled with dyslexia, which at the time was not something the public school system in his small country town of Tokoroa was equipped to adequately accommodate. Because of his unusual athletic talent and his lack of interest in what was offered through mainstream education, he made the choice to drop out of high school and pursue a full-time career in racing. His lifelong dream had always been to move to the United States to race the American Championship, but another interest was to move to Europe to discover if he could hold his own against the world's best racers in the prestigious World Motocross Championship.

With little savings to his name, he decided that Europe was a more viable option, and he set off to make a new life for him-self. After just a few months of singlehandedly carting his motor-cycle around Europe to various events, factory-backed teams soon took notice of this seventeen-year-old's remarkable talent. He soon earned respect among the industry elite and was considered to be a rising star, leading to a full factory sponsorship.

Now equipped with financial backing, it was much easier to dedicate more time to reaching his goal of being at the top of his profession. The culture shock of traveling around Europe was the most difficult learning experience he had ever known, yet expo-sure to this new environment gradually built his character, allow-ing for new understanding of varying mentalities and languages. As the years passed, his talents steadily improved, and he found himself placing remarkably well in events against the world's top seasoned athletes. All seemed well in the world.

Darryl was on a fast track to realizing his dreams of international success when things took an unexpected turn. In 1994, Darryl had been in London speaking with Yamaha in negotiation for the fol-lowing race season and was headed to his next event, an international Supercross in Madrid, Spain. He unbuckled his seatbelt to get more comfortable on the passenger seat and soon fell asleep while his mechanic assumed the responsibility of driving through the night. Darryl awoke to a loud bang. Their rear tire had exploded. Without warning, the vehicle was catapulted into a six-roll spin. He recounts being tossed round and round like a ball bearing in a spray can; the final roll ejected Darryl through the windshield, throwing him onto the opposite side of the freeway. Intense gusts of wind brought on by vehicles passing inches from his head led him to believe this may very well be the end for him. He had landed in the fast lane of the northwest-bound M40 at London's peak rush hour.

Scattered bouts of vague retrospection lend memory of two Good Samaritans who had pulled over and were directing traffic into the middle lane. Darryl recalls a fleeting sense of gratefulness to these strangers as they selflessly kept him from further harm. Meanwhile, Darryl's mechanic's injuries were less critical thanks to the surety of his fastened seatbelt, so at least one of them had been kept relatively stable. Then, after what seemed like a lifetime, emergency vehicles finally arrived. All the while, Darryl was slipping in and out of consciousness due to head trauma and continuous blood loss.

As fate would have it, the crash site was only forty miles north of Oxford University's John Radcliffe Hospital, one of the top medical facilities in the world. The ulna and radius bones within his left arm protruded through his skin, requiring a bone graft from his hip. His right arm had been injured most severely; it had been virtually ripped from his body, attached to his torso by only outer skin, superficial inner tissue, and a few ligaments. Crucial nerves rooted in his spine allocated for mobility of the extremity, including C4, five, and six, had been completely ripped from their attachments.

Oxford's team of top-level nerve-repair surgeons had been called in on the drive from the crash site, and after assessing the damage, they came to a decision: Darryl was to undergo an experimental nerve-reattachment procedure. He was informed of the fifty-fifty chance that amputation might become necessary midsurgery. One of the doctors explained that procedures similar to this had never been documented to grant movement back into the affected extremity, so if he was lucky, the most Darryl could hope for was to possibly have feeling therein after time. It was doubtful that he would ever regain the ability to accomplish anything more than lift a glass of water. And that might only happen after years of therapy—a rarity that was documented in only a very small percentage of cases. The doctor went on to break the news that he would most certainly never have the ability to ride again. This was the end of his career. An immediate rise of emotion prompted Darryl to well up with tears and announce, "I'll prove you wrong."

Fast-forward a few weeks post-op, and Darryl had sold all of his belongings and moved back with his parents in New Zealand. Daily physical therapy sessions had still rendered no voluntary movement of his paralyzed right arm. However, the injury had not affected his hand, so movement of his wrist all the way to the fingertips had been maintained—the sole reason his surgeons had opted not to amputate. With no improvement stemming from his physical therapy efforts, Darryl sought out the top nerve surgeon in New Zealand to have the damage reassessed. His hope was that a new perspective may perhaps give rise to a solution.

Once again, Darryl was given no encouragement. This highly credible medical professional found no hope for the recovery of his arm, a poignant reminder of the devastating news he had been given prior to the initial surgery. Within a few weeks, two more doctors at the top of their field relayed the same news; he was advised to accept his circumstance, to stop chasing the impossible, and to choose a new and less physically demanding career path. In fact, complete surgical removal of the arm was something every one of these doctors urged him to consider. When an arm hangs lifeless, it is very common to develop severe spinal-column damage due to the inevitability of dead weight, resulting in poor, imbalanced posture. The clear realization that no one could offer a solution to bring back his professional racing dreams activated a newfound onset of sheer willpower. He had the choice to give up or to discover an unseen way to somehow beat the odds.

What more could be done other than the regular physical therapy sessions he had been attending a few times each week? He had two good legs, so running was the first thing that came to mind. This simple form of exercise pushed his cardiovascular system, increasing circulation and also offering a therapeutic dose of fresh air. This act of daily outdoor exercise lessened his underlying depression and began to increase his overall strength. Days turned into months, and soon he noticed his arm beginning to periodically twitch and tingle. These subtle movements and distinct sensations were only felt late at night when lying completely relaxed before falling asleep. These sensations undoubtedly meant that progress was being made, albeit rather small and gradual. This brought on a new sense of optimism and was an encouraging factor that urged him to keep moving forward with his self-recovery.

Motocross is ranked among the most physically demanding sports in the world; maneuvering a 250-pound machine around a formidable off-road course requires a tremendous amount of endurance and agility, much of which focuses on upper body strength. The prospect of attempting this seemingly superhuman task was terrifying, but in Darryl's eyes, he had nothing to lose and everything to gain. Just over a year had now gone by since the accident, and he was ready to attempt what his doctors had deemed impossible. Using his left hand to lift and place his right arm onto the handlebar, he grasped with his still-mobile fingers and began to slowly ride around the parking area of his hometown motocross track. A rush of emotion immediately followed. Being back on the bike was the single most gratifying experience he had felt thus far in his life.

Despite frequently losing control of the bike during initial practice sessions, he pushed on and ultimately found himself riding laps and decreasing lap times. He had retrained his neurological pathways to use what once were nerves for breathing to propel his arm into motion. Although his bicep was still not functional, he had gained use of his tricep, which is the most critical muscle needed within the arm to maneuver a motorcycle. He once again began consistently attaining competitive lap times and, after about another year, had reached his goal of returning to a professional level of racing.

Darryl's ability to harness his natural talent and agility rather than brute strength allowed him to ride with fluidity. This disability may have robbed a great deal of his physicality, but he still found himself placing head and shoulders above many accomplished competitors. He went on to win a number of titles, including Czech Republic National Supercross champion and three times Denmark

National champion, and multiple international motocross events, all while sporting an unusual off-center posture due to his partially paralyzed arm.

After moving to the United States in 2003, he won teams champion in the AMA Supermoto Championship, earned eight unlimited main event wins, and placed second in both the 2005 and 2008 championships. All of the 2005 season, he had been leading in overall points. Yet following an unsportsmanlike raceway move outside of his control (brought on by the rider in second position), his rightful first-place position was given to the defending party just meters from the finish line. He had lost the title by a mere two points. Neutral spectators interviewed after this race consider Darryl to be the rightful champion. Tactics used by this aforementioned competitor were both blatantly unclean and treacherous in nature, yet due to biased race-sanctioned politics, these acts were intentionally overlooked by officials. Darryl's humble nature kept him from pursuing justice after his initial attempt of an appeal was denied. This served as another testament to his God-given strength and is an example of yet another conscious choice to remain positive even amid profound adversity. In 2008, he was also leading in overall points throughout the season and lost the championship title by just one point due to a flat tire just two laps from the finish line.

A return to the hospital at Oxford years after his car accident had Darryl's surgeons in awe. As Darryl sat in the cafeteria telling his story of recovery, droves of surgeons, specialists, and medical students gathered around him, intently listening and taking notes. Their experimental surgery had clearly been a success, but they credited the generous output of efforts on his behalf to be the reason for such a positive outcome. The elemental progress of his recovery is detailed in medical textbooks worldwide, and countless procedures of which his doctors pioneered continue to be performed.

As Darryl approached his forties, he chose to bow out of professional racing to pursue the myriad of business ventures he had been presented with. It is often challenging for professional athletes to have the drive and ability to pursue a career in business once they find themselves at the end of their athletic pursuits. Yet the characteristics that had made him successful in racing, as well as the understanding of varying cultures he had acquired during his racing career, now cross over into how he conducts business. This is all despite a lack of formal education due to dyslexia. With the exception of an occasional celebrity event or motivational-speaking engagement, Darryl is now a full-time entrepreneur and business owner, managing global sales relations within the motorcycle industry. Achieving worldwide success, he has earned great respect from colleagues even amid a stressful and fluctuating economic climate.

The next chapter in our story involves the years leading up to my nonvegan pregnancy and the birth of our first son, Elijah, in 2011. Ever since choosing to somewhat renounce plant-based eating in my youth, I had in turn dealt with more health problems than any young person should ever be faced with. In my early- to midtwenties, I was diagnosed and treated with pharmaceutical drugs for depression, social anxiety, and fibromyalgia. To make things worse, I eventually developed symptoms associated with dyspraxia, such as occasional facial paralysis and even a sporadic speech impediment—an unpredictable stutter. A list of additional baffling symptoms too long to include brought me to frequent thoughts of suicide until I was finally "correctly" diagnosed with chronic neurological lyme disease. I use quotes in association with the word *correctly* because I have now become aware that this was only part of my problem; the vast majority of my symptomatology was diet related.

My treatment for lyme was 750mg doxycycline daily for six weeks followed by four weeks of Zithromax, which may have assisted in keeping my disease at bay but also obliterated my microbiome (the critically important network of internal flora that support immune function). Even with therapeutic doses of probiotics, the high levels of antibiotics had brought me to such a heightened state of physical pain and chronic fatigue that I was simply unable to function normally. I had already been severely neglecting relationships with friends and family due to the humiliation of my aforementioned abnormalities, and as years passed, the majority of people I knew had become confused by my reclusion. I did everything in my power to keep people from having to see what I had become, eventually giving up on trying to explain why I would often cancel plans last-minute or avoid social gatherings altogether.

After finding no help from mainstream medicine, I reached out to a number of naturopaths. All of them advised that adding bone broth, wild Atlantic salmon, and grass-fed yogurt (or kefir) into my diet would help to restore my brain function, immune system function, and my gut flora. Upon inquiring about returning to a vegan diet, one naturopathic doctor even proclaimed that all long-term vegans were sickly and that veganism was out of the question if I ever wanted to be healthy.

I was ready to try just about anything to get myself back to a state of normalcy. I deadened my senses and began preparing bone broth, salmon, and kefir for myself. I quickly discovered that even raw, organic dairy was not something that agreed with me and promptly eliminated that. Just a few days into eating the fish and bone broth, I began to notice a slew of uncomfortable side effects that I had never before experienced. Despite these clear warning signs, I continued on this path. My symptoms eventually leveled out, and although I wasn't back to normal, I had concluded that this was as good as it would get—that the way I was feeling was normal. This was just something I had to live with for the rest of my life.

Fast-forward a few years to 2010, and Darryl and I were expecting our first child, Elijah. The beginning of this pregnancy was particularly challenging for me because I suffered from hyperemesis gravidarum (severe morning sickness) and had to deal with hospitalization due to an inability to keep down fluids. Other than frequent lethargy and nausea throughout almost the entirety of my pregnancy, I was a model patient, heeding my obstetrician's advice very closely. I ate the recommended amount of wild Atlantic salmon, and I took prenatal vitamins, fish oil, and iron supplements. At the time, I was completely in the dark about the high toxicity levels of many pharmaceutical-grade prenatal vitamins and iron supplements. I was warned that an old snowboarding injury to my sacrum would render it potentially unsafe for me to deliver naturally, so our beautiful boy came into this world via cesarean section.

As Elijah grew, he was achieving all the normal milestones for the first six months. He had always been very present and alert, even to the point of being extra sensitive, but one day he almost completely ceased eye contact and exhibited unusual repetitive behaviors. At first I thought nothing of this, but as the months wore on, he would move through periods of alarming ups and downs. Most days he would smile and look to us when we called his name, but he began to go through periods of two or three consecutive days where even loud clapping, singing, and sensory experiences that he normally loved did not evoke any sort of response. Then there were the days when ordinary household noises such as a fork tapping against a pot or my husband crumpling up a piece of paper to discard would sporadically bring on bouts of incessant, inconsolable crying; all the while, his eyes took on an unfamiliar glazed-over appearance. This would last for hours until his little body eventually gave in to a deep exhaustion-induced sleep. I had witnessed plenty of juvenile temper tantrums in my day, and this was on an entirely different level. The heartbreak of being utterly helpless and unable to console his agony nearly brought me to mental collapse.

On top of that, he needed antibiotics several times each year for various illnesses, including bronchitis and pneumonia. At two years old, he was diagnosed with the beginning stages of asthma, and after expressing our concerns about his neurological abnormalities, his doctor referred us to an early childhood behavioral specialist. This specialist warned that this was not something children typically grew out of. We were advised to educate ourselves on autism spectrum disorder to gain understanding of available management options and to prepare for the obstacles likely to arise in years to come.

This diagnosis inspired us to go the extra mile to pinpoint what was triggering his basic health and neurological issues. The enigmatic nature of our conundrum was beyond baffling as we really did think we were raising our son in a healthy way—e.g., organic diet and organic living, ayurvedic food, extended breastfeeding, attachment parenting, and the list goes on.

Since I was still breastfeeding at the time, our naturopath advised us both to implement a gluten-free, corn-free diet, which slightly reduced the severity of his health issues but did not resolve them. I was now ready to return to my roots, go against the grain, and experiment with a plant-based diet. I had had enough, and there was nothing I wouldn't do to bring my child to a state of complete health.

Within a few months of eliminating all animal products and their byproducts, Elijah had become the picture of great health. Rarely a runny nose, clear airway passages, and completely free from asthma. He ceased all abnormal behaviors and is considered on-target for his age range—now a very happy and affectionate little boy who hasn't the least bit of interest in nonvegan meal or treat options. When the rare occurrence of illness does present itself, symptoms last for a day or two, and they are extremely mild. Darryl, a lifelong meat lover, has also wholeheartedly adopted a vegan lifestyle. Before considering the evidence, Darryl never would have seriously considered veganism. He regrets not making this dietary shift sooner because he now performs at an even higher athletic level, with significantly quicker recovery times than what he had been able to achieve during his prime racing years in his late teens and twenties. And when adhering to a balanced, low-fat, plant-based, whole-foods diet, I, for the first time in what seems like an eternity, have abundant energy and am asymptomatic with regard to all my previously discussed maladies.

This change fueled curiosity within me, and I began to research a litany of scientific studies that documented the unparalleled benefits of a whole-foods, plant-based diet on human health.[1] I soon discovered that a whole-foods, plant-based diet had not only been shown to dramatically reduce, and in many cases completely eliminate, rise of common diseases but had the clear ability to reverse advanced stages of these diseases as well.

This brought to mind my mother's complete reversal of second-stage cervical cancer at age twenty-four. Through deep prayer and divine intervention, she had been inspired to remove all animal products and processed foods from her diet in an effort to heal.

---

[1] A great place to start your research is with these books: *The China Study* by T. Colin Campbell, PhD, and Thomas M. Campbell II. *Prevent and Reverse Heart Disease* by Dr. Caldwell B. Esselstyn Jr. *Dr. Neal Barnard's Program for Reversing Diabetes* by Neal D. Barnard, MD.

These changes resulted in the remission of her cancer in less than a year's time.

Furthermore, at age eight, a liquid vegan diet played a determining role in reversing trauma I had sustained from a horseback-riding accident that left two-thirds of my liver in hematoma. Doctors warned that rupture was a very real possibility, and the amount of blood loss from such an occurrence would be fatal. Immediate implementation of a liquid vegan diet allowed me to recover quickly, and on the tenth day of hospitalization, an MRI revealed remarkable liver regeneration. The hematoma reduced to one inch in diameter and within a few months' time had fully resolved. My mom honored the cleansing and healing benefits of veganism, but at the time, she was not aware of this diet's ability to sustainably support well-being for a lifetime.

These reminders, on top of the experience with my son, encouraged me to pursue and earn a certification in the field of plant-based nutrition.[2] One course lecture struck me in particular—an analysis of the detrimental, accumulative impacts that animal agriculture is having on both the hunger crisis and the environment. Our current worldwide population is around 7.3 billion,[3] and about one in every nine people on earth is reported to be malnourished.[4] Being confronted with these statistics was quite alarming, and I immersed myself in learning what exactly the predominant factors at the root of this problem are. There must be a more impactful solution than prevalent mainstream recommendations such as recycling, buying electric vehicles, and even population reduction.

Inevitably, all facets of existence are interconnected in a much more profound way than we often realize. Human life, nonhuman animal life, the environment, and so on all intertwine synergistically, meaning our day-to-day choices have the potential to either positively or gravely affect our surroundings. If we all made a decision

[2]   Certified in plant-based nutrition through the T. Colin Campbell Center for Nutrition Studies and Cornell University. http://www.regenerationnetwork.com
[3]   Population Reference Bureau. 2015. 2015 World Population Data Sheet. http://www.prb.org/pdf15/2015-world-population-data-sheet_eng.pdf
[4]   World Food Programme 2015. http://m.wfp.org/hunger/stats (This is a very modest statistic. Unreported malnourished may bring this number closer to half of the population.)

to remove animal products and byproducts from our diet, the above-mentioned number of malnourished people would dramatically decrease. To put this into perspective, let's say that someone chooses to buy one pound of beef for dinner. This single pound requires approximately five thousand gallons of water to produce[5]—this includes only the amount of water used to grow the cow's feed. The quantity of water that would be conserved by eliminating animal products from our diet could be utilized for growing an abundance of plant foods for human consumption. Therefore, we would have the ability and resources to feed each and every hungry mouth, allowing us to significantly decrease crop land loss, soil erosion[6], habitat loss, species extinction, ocean dead zones,[7] and so much more.

I have merely touched on the outskirts of these pressing issues, so I encourage you to delve deeper into all of what I have brought up in these short paragraphs. We as individuals have the power to assist our earth in recovery from this soon-to-be irreparable damage. When we come across people who are prepared to listen, it is our responsibility to openly share this information without judgment and in an altruistic way. Bear in mind that altering one's diet does take time. Remaining patient with yourself and those around you is a crucial factor needed to achieve long-term success.

Together, we can initiate a much-needed paradigm shift toward a holistic health-care model, which will simultaneously set us on the path to a more sustainable future. Shifting one's diet to this extent is commonly perceived as an act of difficile forfeiture and that consumption of animal products is somehow associated with elitism while plant matter is merely reserved for the second-class citizen. For centuries, we have been misled by unfounded assumptions yet have been blessed to be born in an era where change is on the horizon. With this newfound awareness, we will only forfeit disease, assist in the repair of the environment, and renounce the oppression of fellow beings with whom we are privileged to share this planet.

5   Pimentel, D. 2004. Livestock production and energy use. In, *Encyclopedia of Energy*, Matsumura, R. (ed.), Elsevier, San Diego, CA. pages 671–676.

6   Pimentel, D. 2006. Soil erosion: a food and environmental threat. *Environment, Development and Sustainability*. 8: 119–137.

7   Annenberg Learner. https://www.learner.org/courses/envsci/unit/text.php?unit=9&secNum=7
Business Insider 2013. http://www.businessinsider.com/map-of-worldwide-marine-dead-zones-2013-6

Continually envision yourself as an embodiment of the change you wish to see, and in time, repetition of this thinking will guide you, step by step, toward the goals you strive to accomplish.

"There comes a time when one must take a position that is neither safe, nor political, nor popular, but he must take it because his conscience tells him that it is right."

—Martin Luther King Jr.

CHAPTER SEVEN

Venessa Campbell

The Best is Yet to Come

It was just before New Year's 2003. I was getting prepared to go out and celebrate the new year. Trying to figure out what I was going to wear, I went to put my jeans on, and I couldn't get them past my hips. I couldn't believe I couldn't fit in my jeans. At that time velour and terry cloth outfits were the in thing to wear. Needless to say, I hadn't worn a pair of jeans in forever. I decided to weigh myself, and I weighed a whopping two hundred pounds. At that moment I decided to change my life.

I did what I had to do to change my eating habits and start training. I was down by thirty pounds six months later. I was on track with everything. In June 2004 I found out I was pregnant with my son. For the first six months of my pregnancy, I was sick twenty-four hours a day. I didn't gain that much weight my last three months of pregnancy; it was a free-for-all where I could finally enjoy a meal and then some. By the time I delivered, I was 215 pounds. I changed my lifestyle completely after delivery. By my son's first birthday, I was 150.

For years I kept my weight under control by diet and exercise. After years of diet and exercise, I took some time off just to rest. I had been working a lot and was just mentally and physically exhausted. One day someone told me I looked as if I had gained some weight, so I decided to weigh myself. I was back up to 170 pounds, and that was exactly what I had weighed when I found out I was pregnant. Right then and there I decided to get back on track. The difference between when I had lost weight years ago and now was that I was doing it for a man who told me I had gained some weight. I was so obsessed with it that I had gotten so skinny that now this man is telling me I was too skinny now.

I was literally at a standstill. First I was fat, and now I was too skinny. I decided to do some research. I was going through fitness magazines trying to find a program that I loved and could stick with. One night I just so happened to stumble upon a woman in an ad, and I was like, *I want to look like her.* I googled her name, and there she was. I was astonished by how much she had achieved in the fitness industry. At that moment I did more research on Jennifer Nicole Lee and found out so much: She was a mom; she was a weight-loss success story; and she had this incredible, healthy body. I started going through her YouTube channel, and she had these amazing workouts. I figured I had nothing to lose.

After six months of doing JNL Fusion, I transformed my body. I was healthy, I had muscle tone, and I was in the best shape of my life. So with that being said, when I found out she was going to be at Mr. Olympia 2012, I had to meet her. I was able to meet her and talk to her about my weight loss and take some pictures with her. Jennifer was sweet and charismatic. I have met plenty of celebrities, but I was more excited to meet Jennifer than anyone else. Jennifer changed my life when it came to health and fitness and made such a positive impact.

In the last couple of years, I had some injuries that caused me to take time off from training. I've been back on track for the last couple of months since JNL has been at her studio online. I download her workouts and have them right there at my fingertips. I am able to train anywhere at any time, so there are no excuses. The last twelve years have been a journey for me to say the least, and the best is yet to come.

CHAPTER EIGHT

by Barbara Server-Busch

"I AM ENOUGH"

It was a February morning in 2008. I woke with a burning desire to make change. To make a change in my lifestyle. I was tired, fat, and broken. I had been praying for an answer—a solution. I picked up a book that was going to show me how—I read it, told my trainer that this was how we were going to train, and I lived it for twelve weeks. I started making friends in the gym, one of whom was Lisa. One time she came up to me and asked me to do a figure competition. *Hmm. What's that?* I asked my trainer what she thought, and right away without a blink, she said, "*Yes,* you need to do this." Training started August 1 for an October 1 show. I ate what she told me to, slept when she told me to, and drank how much she told me to. I stepped on that stage October 1, 2008, and took first place in the novice category, second in masters (forty-five and over). Here's the kicker: I was forty-eight years old with thyroid issues, in full-blown menopause, and having extreme digestive issues, but I did it and *loved* it. I had always wanted to be on stage as Miss America, and this was close enough for me...

My business was growing, as was my passion for helping others live a healthy lifestyle. I was building my nutrition business behind the chair as a hairstylist, but there was one problem: my clients were tired, and I was tired. Chopping, prepping, cooking, packing, measuring five to six meals a day times seven was exhausting, but I know there wasn't anything better than what I was putting on our plates; I wasn't into supplements. My clients were frustrated and leaving my program, so I started my research, something that would give us energy without additives, preservatives, artificial sweeteners, and digestive enzymes. I found it, the right company to give me the products that would help with what we all needed, and *bam*, there it was. I had my motivation back, weight and inches were falling off, and I actually had muscle.

I thought I had it all, that I had the world by the tail. I was happy, fulfilled, and successful. Just what every girl wants, right? Nope! There were a couple of pieces of this puzzle missing. I was unhappy in my marriage, realized I didn't love myself enough to take better care of *me*, and was exhausted with no energy. So out comes another book; this one is called *The Secret*. I read it, and that's when I learned if I don't love myself, I cannot give love. That book was followed by another, and another one after that. Soon I was feeling as if I had superpowers. I had gained control of my feelings. I was loving me again, enough to admit that my marriage had failed, and we split. We had been together for thirty-six years, married for twenty-seven. I was devastated but knew deep down it was the best for both of us.

In June 2011, I was told I needed shoulder surgery—damage from repetitive motion from doing hair for thirty years. Between losing the income from my career and marriage, I was scared. What was I going to do? Both were all I knew. Personal development was really helping me stay focused and believe that I could do anything I desired. Just put it out to the universe, and it will come back to you. Fruition. OK, wow, this is really cool. I was liking what was happening, so I called the girls who I enrolled in the nutrition company I was with and told them I was ready to get into the industry of network marketing full time but that I needed guidance. *That* was it. I found it. I found that missing puzzle piece. I honestly had *no* idea this life was waiting for me—what a blessing. I moved away and started my life over, by myself, for myself, and my business flourished. Eighteen months later I was a six-figure earner in this company and learned that 89 percent of women who make a six-figure income do it in network marketing. Wow, how awesome did that feel to be a statistic of something really great? I was happier than I had ever been in my entire life and fell in love with myself. Because of that I met the most amazing man who, four and a half years later, is now my husband. Together we have four children, a son-in-law, and three grandbabies. We travel when we want, where we want, and we absolutely love life.

My name is Barbara Busch, and *I am enough*.

CHAPTER NINE

Jennifer Lowe-Nazradi

The Power of a Sunflower

It was a brisk fall day in Marshall. Fallen leaves sprinkled the damp roads, lush lawns, and pointed roofs of the quiet town where we lived, draping all in a quilted blanket of reds, oranges, and yellows with just a hint of pale green. The distinct aroma of Michigan autumn permeated the atmosphere, blending the scent of freshly cut grass with the smoky musk of dry leaves and distant bonfires. I inhaled the bouquet, heeding its olfactory warning. I knew that I better enjoy that gentle fall chill and summer's last bit of lingering warmth, for Old Man Winter would soon be blowing into the Great Lakes region, preserving the town in a frosty time capsule during the long winter that lay ahead.

I relished the crisp air swirling around me, the scent of that familiar autumn potpourri infusing my smooth strawberry-blond locks as I unleashed every bit of might in my six-year-old body to propel my purple Schwinn Starlight at top speed. I was confident that my bike was the best one around. It was my vehicle for escaping the world. The faster I rode, the better. I loved the way the wind would scramble through my hair, tangling it as only a furious breeze could do. I loved to pretend, and my imagination was at its most colorful when I was speeding on my bike. I would dream of my future and what it might entail. I would embody characters I knew from movies and TV, or I'd make up my own. The swiftness and intensity of flying on my bike only made the personifications of my imagination more vivid. Today I was the Wicked Witch of the West in *The*

Wizard of Oz. I rode faster, laughing to myself with my best evil witch cackle. The white stars that speckled my bike were surely just blurry streaks to neighbors who were outside raking their lawns as I whizzed past. I rode high on the pedals, exhilarated, barely touching the banana seat as I lapped our cul-de-sac in record time.

Before I knew it, Dad was flagging me down in an effort to get me to stop riding and come inside for dinner. I skidded into the driveway at a sharp angle and hopped off reluctantly. The noisemakers on my spokes that were shaped as miniature soda cans made a tinkling noise as I walked the bike into the front yard. I ditched my bike and bounced up the driveway with the assuredness of a little girl who knows she's pretty darn cute. My face was a representative combination of my two parents. There was no mistaking me for anyone else's child. I had the almond-shaped eyes of my Japanese father and the nose, cheeks, and chin of my mother, who is 100 percent Polish. A distinct mole sat in perfect placement over my upper lip. It stayed the same size as my face grew, so it's less prominent now, but at the time, it was quite noticeable. To me, it was the ultimate beauty mark.

You see, it was 1987. Madonna had released her album *True Blue* the year before, and her movie *Who's That Girl* had just been released that summer. All things Madonna were in with young girls at the time. We wore bangles, scrunched our hair, and based almost every fashion decision on what Madonna would do. Upper lip moles were a necessity, and I just so happened to be naturally blessed with the signature of America's biggest pop icon. I couldn't have asked for more. The other girls at school had to fake it by drawing one on their face with black eyeliner. Beyond the mole, I had smooth and flawless light-olive skin. Lanky and tall for my age, I even towered over some of the boys in my class at school. Since my baby teeth had fallen out early, adult teeth grew in before my mouth could grow to accommodate them. This gave me an unusually large smile for someone my size. I was adorable, and I enjoyed being me.

I could entertain myself for hours. Aside from portraying characters while speeding on my bike, I loved the imaginary worlds of movies and television. My favorite cartoons were *The Smurfs*,

Gummy Bears, and *Inspector Gadget*. I was obsessed with Barbie dolls and My Little Pony. Of course, *The Wizard of Oz* was my favorite movie. I still know every word of dialogue in it to this day. I watched it constantly and naturally acquired a childhood obsession with Judy Garland. I was so taken with her performance, in fact, that I wanted to change my name to Dorothy. I would tell my friends, my family, and everyone I met to call me Dorothy. My request was often laughed off as silly and childish, but I was quite serious. I didn't like my name at the time because there were three to five Jennifers in every classroom at school. My father finally told me that the reason he chose the name Jennifer was because he found it to be the most beautiful of all the girls' names he had ever heard. That did it, and I started to forget about changing my name. From that point on, I thought of it as a nice gesture from my father. I still identified with Dorothy, though, much due to the recurring theme "There's no place like home" because I felt exactly the same way.

From my perspective, I had the ideal little family and a sublime life. First of all, I had two loving parents. Plus, I had two younger brothers who were both healthy. We were spaced out perfectly—all three years apart. Since I was six at the time, Chris was three, and Cyle was almost one. It worked out nicely so that we all got our own quality time with my dad. Life was good for us. Some of my friends had a sick sibling, or they only had one parent at home, so I appreciated what I had.

I was happy and content, which gave me the security and strength to be independent. I would find a way to do what I wanted to do, no matter what. I loved to delve into imaginary worlds and personas. As a child, I spent an inordinate amount of time daydreaming about maturing from a little girl into a young woman. I contemplated how I would act as an adult, what kind of car I would drive, who I would marry. I had a Cinderella wedding all planned out in my head by the time I turned twelve. One of my idols at the time was Punky Brewster. I admired her creativity and thought she was super-cool in general. One day I went to school with two different shoes on, pulled back my hair into two pigtails, and wore a handkerchief wrapped around my right knee. The teacher called my mother at home and asked why she had let me go to school looking like that. Mom didn't know what I had done because I had secretly changed on the walk to school. I found the situation hilarious. I vividly recall other instances where I pretended that I was English like Mary in *The Secret Garden*. I would imagine that I was in the garden that she could never reach, and I would run around exploring it and admiring its beauty. Other times, I would turn an everyday playground set into a fortress sitting on a cliff surrounded by a stone wall. I would be the princess and the ruler of my kingdom, my backyard garden, and my horse-and-carriage sandbox chariot. I was a little girl who would always take long bike rides with my friends, run around in the front yard, have tea parties with my teddy bears, swing on the swings, and play make-believe with my friends and stuffed animals. I also loved to read. To me, any book was a good book as long as it told a good story.

Though I had friends my age to play with, my best friend was my father. Half-Japanese and half-English, he considered himself to be an American mutt. He had thick black hair that he wore neatly combed back with an inch of volume on the top. He spoke through his actions and his eyes, which were deeply sincere. They were almond shaped and a dark chestnut brown, indicative of his Japanese descent. His eyes gave away his feelings. When he smiled, he would squint, emanating an amused wisdom. When he was happy or pleased with something, I'd notice a twinkle in his eye. He was funny, sweet, and stern when necessary. He loved his children, and we meant everything to him. He was our hero and mentor. We wanted to be wise like him. He was not a man of many words, so when he voiced his opinion, we listened. He spoiled me with his love and affection, and I relished every single second of it. I looked up to him. I knew I could count on him for anything. With him, I felt content, happy, and complete. I knew I was lucky to have such a wonderful father, but I didn't realize just how fortunate I was until I saw the way other parents treated their kids. Many fathers were not around much in the 1980s. Some of my friends' fathers worked constantly, acting more as providers than as father figures. Others were absent and caught up in their own lives. Mine worked eight to four so he could make it home by four thirty in the afternoon for our quality time. We had so many adventures together: going to the beach, visiting the state park, fishing, or going to the movies. We would dabble in hobbies or go to the toy store to reward good behavior. We would do anything that allowed us to appreciate and enjoy life. At the park, it was all about "twirly" slide, which was my name for the slides that curved around and spiraled all the way to the ground. When we'd drive past a park that had one, I would ask my father to stop for me. He would do it every time. He was always doing whatever it took to make me happy. He was the father who would push me on the merry-go-round until I was nauseous because he seemed to enjoy making me laugh and smile until I couldn't take it anymore. He fed off my happiness and laughter, and I adored him for that.

He was also a man of great wisdom and smarts where life was concerned. He taught me to be who I am today. He taught me to speak when necessary and to honor the earth. He was fascinated with nature and had a deep respect for it. He endowed me with the Golden Rule, and I still abide by it today. I can almost hear him saying, "Just treat people the way you want to be treated." It was from my father that I learned to pause before speaking to think about what I was going to say and how the other person might feel should I decide to share. That simple life lesson has made me who I am. I credit my father's wisdom when people tell me that I am very genuine and sweet. I treat others that way simply because it's how I would like to be treated. Besides, I think that life's too short to be angry or spiteful.

My father had a special appreciation for trees. To him, they were simple elements of nature that replenished his soul. Pine trees, oak trees, birch trees—if you can name a tree, my father loved it. Trees make it possible for us to breathe. My father felt that we must give thanks to them as we would not exist in their absence. "They are a part of our makeup and a part of the living whole," he would say. There was a certain poem my father would read to me, exhibiting that sincere squint of wisdom as he read it. I distinctly remember the last line because I thought it was a little silly yet full of truth: "Poems are made by fools like me, but only God can plant a tree." When he read that poem, I could tell that he thought the words were perfectly integrated together to describe the importance of one of Mother Nature's most precious endowments, the gift of fresh air that allows us to live and breathe. My father loved planting trees. To him, it was a hobby and a labor of love. A natural landscaper and somewhat of a natural farmer at heart, he was very good at it.

Following Dad's lead, I too began to have a love affair with nature's gifts. I would spend the dark Michigan winters looking forward to springtime when we would go to the nursery to plant our garden. My father didn't plant the standard rectangular garden like our friends and neighbors. He enjoyed being creative, working the garden into the design of the home and property and complementing the landscape. We had a typical backyard with a fence around the border. My father would dig up the soil around the outside of the fencing so that the garden outlined our yard. We placed starter tomato plants in the ground around the fence along with seeds for green beans, pumpkins, cucumbers, red and green peppers, strawberries, and raspberries. We watered and waited and watered and waited and waited and watered. Weeks later, Mother Earth bore life to reward our hard work. Our little Midwestern fence garden was one of the most bountiful I've ever seen. It was incredibly rewarding that we had grown all of it by ourselves, and we could eat from the roots of our backyard. To me it seemed like a miracle granted by God.

That spring, I had specifically picked out a seed pack for sunflowers. I liked them because they grew so tall and looked so happy. To me, the sunflowers were the most important part of the garden. I adored the way they seemed so delighted to be given life. More so, they were taller than I was as they stood about four and a half feet tall. I was amazed that a flower could be as large as a small tree. Their magnitude enhanced their beauty even more, and I liked to think of them as supermodels with long legs. To me, sunflowers were appreciative, and I had a deep admiration for them. I liked to watch them sway with the wind, slightly bending as though they were bowing to us for the right we had given them, the right to life. They would lift up their leaf arms to the sun as it shone on them to give thanks and praise to the light for which we sometimes do not remember to be thankful. Every time I see a sunflower today, I get that same feeling of accomplishment, of tender and sweet contentment. I will cherish and cultivate that feeling within me for the rest of my life, for I find it incredible that something so simple can bring a person such rejuvenation.

CHAPTER TEN

"My Inspirational Story" by Dina Conforti

I spent years working on myself, cleaning up my insides, forgiving myself, refocusing, letting go of fear, and dealing with my anxiety. I had no choice. Fear had taken over, and my anxiety was so intense that I started to get really bad chest pains that would wake me during the night.

Fast forward ten years, and my life was still not perfect, still filled with life-changing experiences, but I was different. I was balanced, happy, and peaceful inside. Chest pains were a thing of the past.

Then I had children.

Two in two years. Suddenly, I no longer knew who I was and found myself questioning every single thing in my life. I couldn't make the simplest decisions, always turning to others to see what they thought was best. Constantly second-guessing every thought, action, and reaction. How exhausting!

Add seventy-five pounds of weight to my five-foot-tall, petite figure, and now we had one messed-up woman. *Who is that in the mirror looking back at me?* I thought to myself as my daughter screamed for me and my son raced to tell me he wanted something to drink. I had only a few seconds each day to think to myself, let alone do anything for myself.

It will come, don't stress, I reminded myself... *Yes, but when? I'm tired of feeling like this!*

I was fed up of wearing clothes to hide certain parts of me. A bra had used to be optional for me. After breastfeeding two kids and pumping exclusively for many months straight, believe me, those perky breasts were long gone!

Any woman who has gone through this can relate. We watch our partners go about life with very little, if any, physical changes at all, and this spurs our crazy, unbalanced hormones to scream in frustration even more. I know some moms who have had very little weight gain and whose bodies didn't go through drastic changes like mine did. That is great for them; really, I am happy for them. These words I am writing are not for those moms; they are reaching out to the two-hundred-pound women who are fed up and want change.

Being five feet tall and carrying two-hundred-plus pounds is a terrible feeling. Knees hurt, back hurts, joints hurt. Simple activities become uncomfortable, some impossible, and suddenly you're buying slip-on shoes because you don't want to go through the hassle of attempting to bend over and tie laces.

I promised myself that after breastfeeding I would start to do something about my weight. I had to. I was starting to become miserable and self-conscious. Speaking with my husband, I contemplated joining the gym again or buying a treadmill. Living in Montreal means lots of snowy days, and getting lazy can be easy.

So the gym was a no-go because I have very little free time during the day as I'm usually completing a million chores and taking care of two kids while my husband works. On the rare occasion I find time, I would rather try to catch up on sleep. I'm always so beat by the end of the day.

The treadmill was way too expensive, not to mention way too big. So there I was frustrated with myself because the gym seemed to be the only option, but realistically I knew I could never get a chance to go.

My son will soon be three, and my daughter is twenty months. I have very little help with them during the day and no one whom I can just drop the kids off to. It's a tough job, and it can get overwhelming. I can honestly say that I have not had a night out with friends or a date night with my husband in almost four years…I'm just too tired.

Why am I going on and on about all of this? Because I found just what I needed with Jennifer Nicole Lee! I prayed and asked the universe to help me find an outlet. I knew that if I could get back to feeling great, as I did before having kids, I would be a better wife and mom. I desperately wanted it!

That's when I found JNL's e-gym that was offering online classes at www.JNLFitnessStudioOnline.com Not knowing exactly what that was and knowing for certain I could never attend a live class due to my crazy schedule, I decided to send an e-mail to get further informed. Well, the response was quick, and the answer was perfect! I was able to purchase and download the class, keep it forever, and do it whenever I could…Yes! Thank you, universe! Thank you, gorgeous and talented Jennifer Nicole Lee! You're an angel; this was my saving grace!

I started with one workout and became addicted. Able to do it whenever I can, in my home, and wearing whatever I want gives me the chance to really focus on myself and my workout. Jennifer goes a step further and talks to your higher self the entire time. She feeds that positivity to your soul, which makes the workouts fly by! Before you know it, you are in the shower feeling amazing, grateful, and blessed for everything in your beautiful life.

I started my first workout in mid-May. I have tried my best to be consistent and work out three days a week, but it's so addictive—I swear I wish it were my job—I now do four to five workouts a week. I wish I could do four or five a day; they are just too good! My body is slowly transforming, and I'm feeling so much stronger than I did just under two months ago.

My abs, my poor abs, took a beating in two years. I had two very big pregnancies, two very big babies (no gestational diabetes), which resulted in two cesareans. Not to mention two blood transfusions with my son's delivery—but that's another story in itself.

That's quite a bit to recover from. Believe me when I tell you that I was very weak afterward. I could not lift my legs when lying flat. But now…Woo-hoo! I am doing all sorts of different ab exercises. I could have hardly done one before, and today I'm doing the fifteen-minute ab videos—of course, still with some struggle, but I'm doing it!

I see so much progress in such a short time. The best feeling is when someone says, "Wow, you're looking great!" It just confirms it even more.

It has been only two months, and the transformation is amazing! I am finally starting to see the person I was come back in that mirror.

I am very grateful to have found JNL workouts! We are so lucky to have this opportunity. This is stuff the celebrities pay big money for, and it's available with all the extra bells and whistles for only a few dollars! Jennifer, thank you, thank you, thank you for doing this! You are not only helping me but my kids, my husband, and all those around me because I am transforming, exuding beautiful vibes that spread to all those in my life. So from the bottom of my heart, thank you!

CHAPTER ELEVEN

"Now I Have a Vision," by Laura Conforti

Six years ago I had my one and only son—the golden child, we call him. After many years of trying and a few miscarriages, *my* pride and joy was born! I thought my weight before the pregnancy was high, but it was nothing compared to the weight I put on afterward. Nothing prepared me for the depression and hunger I felt. Nothing filled the emptiness I felt. My husband worked nights, and I felt mostly alone and afraid. My comfort was my food. Breastfeeding was my excuse, fear, me being overly tired, loneliness, depression. I had every excuse in the book, I still do! I tried it all: Weight Watchers, Atkins, Fit Tea, and Whole30. All worked wonders.

Then you stop, and *boom*, back up again. I must have started this journey a million times so far in my forty-three years of life. What's different now? This time I started with my physical body and not my mind. That came automatically without a large struggle. Let me explain: Usually I would read up on diets and learn and follow using my brain, mostly controlling what I ate. This time around I said I'd try something different. Thanks to my sister Dina, I was introduced to Jennifer, JNL, and things have slowly begun to change.

I jumped right into a workout routine, which made me feel awesome, and then another one, and that dessert didn't look so good, but I ate it and thought, *Tomorrow I'm burning it off*. And I did! By the third and fourth workout, I didn't want dessert. I was on a roll, getting rid of my rolls. By the second week, I was brimming with energy to the point where others noticed. I started spreading the word at work, and a couple of people joined in.

Then I lost all motivation, got down, stopped working out, started eating, and now I'm back up again...

But wait. Did I forget how good I felt working out? Why did I stop? Renovations, painting, no room, work, life... *It's OK,* I thought to myself. *Laura, you got this.*

This is forever, so one or two weeks are not going to change things. Losing myself for a couple of days or weeks is OK because I will jump right back into it again, and this is what counts. It's a lifestyle change. Now I'm working out because it makes me feel good and look good, and I love it!

Thank you, Jennifer, for making me *love* working out.

Now I have a vision. It's faint, but I see it there in the back. It's coming into focus. My dream is to get to a completely fit body and start working for you, motivating and becoming an image of what love for oneself is—what a real woman is!

Lots of love,

Laura

CHAPTER TWELVE

Nikki Kerivan

Never Stop Dreaming

I'm Nikki. I'm not your average thirty-year-old. I'm full of positive energy and adventure, and I truly believe you should live your life with kindness in your heart and your eyes open to the world around you. To say I've always been this way would be the truth. My story isn't how I became this way; it's how I remained this way after the speed bumps I've hit in my life. I was raised in a household of dreamers, where nothing was unreachable. Where integrity, hard work, and believing in yourself were the ways to accomplish your dreams. Both of my parents and my sister never gave up on anything they set out to do, and I never have either.

Some of my life's trials so far would include an attack on my eighteenth birthday (one I still suffer from with PTSD, which I strive to help others overcome), losing my home in Hurricane Katrina, and most recently coming to find that with improper nutrition and coaching you can lose your health and even your faith in achieving a goal. Aside from my rough experiences, I have so many things to be thankful for. My family, my husband, and my unchanging faith that everything will work out if you believe it will.

To tell you the details of my trials was something I needed to prepare myself for. Displaying your toughest days isn't something you do for fun but something you do to hopefully bring inspiration to someone else out there going through what you've already survived. As with human nature, even the toughest people need someone to look up to, need answers, and sometimes need help. I have found that your mind-set (being the hardest thing to overcome) can be your knight in shining armor or your darkest enemy. You have the power to turn even your worst experiences into something to be learned from and to accept, as long as you believe that you aren't alone and something good is coming your way.

To give you my first of a few stories I'm going to share, I should warn you that it is the most traumatic experience of my life. I still suffer from the PTSD it has caused me, and I still have days when I feel lost. However, I push through those days and believe that whatever the reason is, this happened, and I was meant to do some good in the world with it. I absolutely hate using that one word that defines this experience, but for my readers I'll use it anyway. The word you're probably guessing is correct. Simply put, during my senior year of high school, I was raped. I won't go into details because I am fully aware of how that can make a person feel, but on the night of my eighteenth birthday, I was attacked by a boy at school, and I spent what should have been a rite-of-passage birthday in the hospital. Not a day goes by that I don't suffer from this in some way. I have my own ways of coping with my PTSD and have tried multiple avenues to find a "cure." However, I've come to find that the only cure is being surrounded by loving, positive people and that it takes time. Since my attack I have come to meet so many amazing women who suffer from the same experience and have learned that everyone handles their recovery in so many different ways. Between the tornado of police, nurses, family, friends, courthouses, and lawyers, I want you to know that if you are in the thick of something similar, it will get better. You will be OK, and you will have closure at some point in your life.

As I'm writing this chapter hoping to inspire others to always see the light surrounding them, I'm remembering that today is the day of the year when my life changed. On August 29, 2005, Hurricane Katrina slammed the Gulf Coast with her fury and washed away the life that most of us had come to love. The beautiful home I grew up in rested on the north shore of New Orleans in a town called Slidell. Slidell was the place I grew up, and our home held some of my happiest memories as a kid. I can still remember the day before she hit our coast: watching the hurricane tracker on the news and waiting to see if the headache of evacuating was still the only option. As the storm approached, my family, along with all our pets and our closest friends, gathered up anything of heartfelt value and anything necessary to survive and headed to the neighboring town of Lafayette. That night I remember watching the graphics of this monster hurricane swallow up any view I had of our hometown and the surrounding areas on the map, praying my house was still standing. We lived on couches for a week in the home of someone we barely knew, someone who was kind enough to allow all of us to have shelter as we waited out this storm. The next morning we all walked outside to take in the scenery. Lafayette wasn't under the eye of the storm. However, it was close enough for the weather to take full effect on trees and power lines. I will never forget standing in this residence we evacuated to, trying to call anyone I could reach to find out if anyone was harmed or had an update on our neighborhoods back home. The cell phone signals took me back to September 11, when the news revealed that no one was able to reach family due to the cell phone signals being nonexistent. Over the next few days, our team of dads made their way to Slidell using back roads and a satellite phone to assess the damage and prepare for our return. I can still picture waiting in that living room and watching the news show roofs littered with residents in the New Orleans area. My heart was pounding. Was this what my dad would find when they reached our home? Or did, by the grace of God, our home survive?

Well, our home did not survive Hurricane Katrina. However, by the grace of God, our friend's home did, and because of this, along with their kindness and love, my family had a temporary home while we rebuilt. You see, Hurricane Katrina was the worst storm in our country's history. Lives were lost, homes were swept into the Gulf of Mexico, and families like mine were left homeless and jobless. At the time I was attending the University of New Orleans, and due to my school flooding, my education was put on hold while the city rebuilt. However, I graduated with my bachelor of arts in broadcasting just a year later than I would have. Homes were flooded, but neighbors picked up shovels and gloves and helped their friends rebuild their homes and their lives. Something of this magnitude tore a lot of lives apart, but it also brought so many more lives together. I personally realized what was really important in life, and my eyes were open to how kind friends and strangers can be to one another. It made me realize how blessed I am that, yes, my home was lost forever—something that to this day brings a tear to my eye—however, in the same moment, my family and the people I loved were unharmed.

In the wake of Hurricane Katrina, I learned so much about life. I learned the kindness of strangers. I learned the strength that people have deep inside to overcome such a tragedy. I learned the pride people have in the lives they lead at home, while learning that some have no pride at all. Those who saw value in what they had worked to exhaustion to rebuild their homes and help their neighbors, while some only took what was given to them and left the rest for others to worry about. Life was not made to simply breeze through; life is a journey to learn and grow from. That is what the experience of Hurricane Katrina taught me: that no matter how much rebuilding lies ahead, if you keep pushing forward with kindness and purpose, anything is possible.

Finally, I want to share my most recent speed bump because it has greatly affected where I am today. The fitness industry is extremely rewarding and challenging; many want to be involved, and those with the determination to work hard are the ones who come the closest to reaching their goals. I have been working toward becoming published as a fitness model for years, and once I made the move to the Boston area, it finally dawned on me that I needed to find something different from the sports I was involved in growing up to get there. I needed to find a sport that allowed me to continually improve as a person as well as reach my other goals surrounding it. That is when I came across competing as a bikini and fitness model. I had never done anything like this before, and for my preparation to become stage ready, I needed all the guidance I could get. After speaking with a few other athletes about this, I was convinced joining a competition prep team was the best way to go. My first show was absolutely amazing. I worked extremely hard to earn my place on that stage, made my husband proud, and had pushed myself further than anything I've ever attempted. Because my initial experience was so amazing and I didn't have the knowledge to understand what I was doing to my body, I decided to remain with this team for another upcoming show, hoping to earn my professional status and compete as a pro in future shows. Little did I know that the process I was repeatedly convinced to trust was actually hurting my body on a daily basis. Three weeks before my second show, I became extremely sick and fatigued and reached out for help, but neither of my coaches was there for me. I immediately found a new coach and had help getting my health back in time to step onstage. I was nowhere near stage ready, but at that point my goal was to finish what I had started and work on my health as soon as it was over. I found out shortly after making this switch that I was being overworked and underfed, a common problem when working with a team due to the amount of athletes being trained at the same time. After my second show, I decided to take a break, regain my health, and then train for my next show with my new coach.

My point for telling you these stories isn't to show you how things can go wrong but to inspire you to keep moving forward no matter what comes your way. Every experience happens for a reason. Every loss, every illness, every disappointment; without them you cannot grow as a person. Aside from these rough experiences, I have so many blessings to be thankful for, like my family and my husband who love me unconditionally and my unchanging faith that everything happens for a reason and everything will work out if you believe it will. So what are some of my accomplishments through these life-changing inconveniences? Well, I dreamed of working for the Walt Disney Company since I was a kid; I did it and brought happiness to others while fulfilling my dream and making some of my favorite memories. I worked as hard as I could to become a Boston Bruins Ice Girl for the NHL, and despite not making the team my first time around, I came back and finished out two seasons with an amazing team and experiences to last a lifetime. I graduated college with my bachelor of arts in broadcasting despite my school and my home flooding in one of our country's biggest natural disasters. My husband and I own our own gym now—a dream we both shared—and are giving people the tools they need to accomplish their goals. And now? Well, now I am working toward my third WBFF bikini competition, chasing my dream of going pro and landing my first magazine cover when I am meant to. I don't see my PTSD, the loss of my home, or my once-working metabolism as reasons to not push forward. I see them as learning experiences, and they motivate me not to take the time I've been given in my life for granted. Will I barrel over more speed bumps along the way? Of course; this is life, but they will never slow me down. Always be humble, always be thankful for who you have in your life, always believe in yourself, and never stop dreaming.

A wise man once said, "All our dreams can come true, if we have the courage to pursue them" (Walt Disney). With the support of loved ones and the ability to dream, anything is possible.

CHAPTER THIRTEEN

Candi Taylor

Running to Remember

By the age of ten, I already had broken both arms and had my teeth knocked out. Yes, life was already throwing me curveballs. I learned very early that life is difficult, but you have to stay positive and move forward each day with a grateful heart.

My family and I were always doing something. Be it camping, boating, horseback riding, gocarting, or attending a festival, we were always busy. The family trip to River Ranch was always fun because we had so many things to do at the campsite. We would go hiking, then go swimming, and then watch the rodeo and play in the saloon; there was never a dull moment. One time when I was about five years old, my dad was returning from a fishing trip, and to me it seemed he had been gone for a long time. I heard the adults talking about someone who had come back and was on the boat ramp. My mom shouted out to me and my siblings, "Let's go see what Dad has caught for dinner." I wanted to see him and was excited to find out what he had caught. I ran toward the dock, wanting to be the first to see him. I ran until I seen the end of the fishing dock and jumped right off, screaming, "Dad, catch me!" Well, I had never told anyone I was going to jump off the dock, nor did I know if my dad was going to catch me. I leaped off that dock, and all I seen was my dad's back as he was facing the opposite direction. I went face-first into the concrete boat dock and busted my teeth right out. Everyone ran to me as I was crying and holding my face. There was blood all over the place, and it was dripping from my mouth and face. I reached my hand out along the pavement to retrieve the shattered bits of teeth. My dad picked me up and asked me, "Why in the world would you jump to me without telling me?"

Earlier in the day, a man had told me to jump off the dock, that it would surprise my dad when he returned. The man was not around when all of this took place. Nor did I know who he was. I was so excited to see my dad, and I couldn't wait to surprise him. Some lady brought me a washcloth with ice since my face seemed to be swelling. Everyone was in a panic, and I was at the center of it. Who was the man who had told me to jump off the dock? My stomach ached from swallowing so much blood, and I was sick from the pain of my shattered teeth. We had to travel to find a dentist, and it was a long drive. When we did find a dentist, he told my parents and me my entire upper row of teeth had to be surgically removed. A long and painful process started until all the segments of shattered teeth were taken out. My jaws hurt frequently, and the long healing process unfolded over the next few months. My face was swollen, and I did not look like myself. My speech had even changed. It was a struggle to eat, speak, or even smile. The seasons changed and time moved on, and I started my first year of school at Pinecrest Elementary. I remember praying for my teeth to grow in. Every day I would look in the mirror for a hint of an adult tooth, but it took a while because my gums were damaged.

We lived on a dirt road, and the only time we would have traffic on our road was when the farm crew was arriving or leaving for the day. We never had any issues with the cars or crew normally. Most of the cars took it slow and were courteous. However, the last few cars on that day were obnoxious, and people were screaming, "*Hot* tamales," and other random comments while hanging out the passenger side of a dingy rusty car. All the commotion spooked our horses. My sister Dawn was on a quarter horse in front of me, and as a car drove by and beeped and someone yelled out the window, my horse was startled, raised up his front legs, and kicked his rear legs in the air. Grasping frantically for the horn of the saddle, I tried my best to hold on, but the girth broke. My saddle and I went flying in the air, and I was abruptly introduced to Mother Earth's cold shoulder.

The wind was knocked out of me, and it was hard to breathe. Dawn was still on her horse, and she was OK.

She immediately jumped down and ran over to me. "Are you OK?" All I could do was cry and hold my wrist tight to manage the horrible pain I was feeling. She told me I was going to be OK but that we needed to get help.

Sobbing, I begged her, "Do not leave me by myself." As she was trying to help me, Double O Seven ran down the street. Time seemed to stop. All I could feel was the horrible throbbing and ache in my chest. Everything was blurry around me. I could not squeeze my hand hard enough; I just wanted it to stop hurting. The next thing I remember is looking up and seeing my dad approaching on Double O Seven.

The horse had run back to our house, and my dad had noticed I was not on it. He ran out and jumped on the horse, and Double O brought him to my sister and me. My dad jumped off, scooped me up, and started to carry me home. The entire way he was telling me it was going to be OK and to let go of my wrist. My mom was telling my sister to hurry up and that we were going to the hospital. My dad asked me to stop holding my wrist so tight that it was making my hand turn blue. It hurt so bad that I could not let go of my wrist; holding it was the only thing I could do to help ease the discomfort. As we arrived at the hospital, the lady asked my parents questions and told me she was going to take me to equipment that was going to "look inside my body." Lots of people were asking my parents questions, and I was scared as I had never been to a hospital.

The next few hours are a blur for me. The next thing I remember is waking up in an enclosed crib with plastic around it. A nurse walked up, and I asked where my mom and dad were. She told me they would be in shortly. I was not feeling well, and my arm was wrapped up in this hard material. I could hardly move. My mom finally walked in and told me I was going to be in the hospital for a few days. I wasn't allowed to eat anything—only food through my IV. She told me I needed to rest. My mother told me I had lost some blood and that they had to put more blood inside me. I had to have a blood transfusion to have my elbow repaired. The doctors and nurses had to monitor me for a few days until my fever went away. I was not allowed out of the enclosed crib until my fever was gone and my blood count was where it was supposed to be. I was scared and hungry. The nurse walked into the room after I had been asking several times for food and told me she had french fries for me. I was so excited; I could finally eat. But to my dismay, she was joking and had a bag of clear IV fluid. I was weak and not happy about being locked in the crib and did not like the nurse after that.

They had to insert two metal pins in my elbow to repair the damage. They were sticking out of my arm. Finally after a week or so, my body was starting to heal, and my fever went away. While it was healing, I did not let a cast keep me down. I still wanted to do everything I was used to doing, including climbing trees. I would climb with my cast and hang from the tree branch. Yes, I was very active and thought I could do anything. Even with a broken arm and toothless grin, I was determined to enjoy myself and live life to the fullest. After my arm was healed, it was time to remove the pins from my elbow. My mom and my grandma Betty took me to get the pins removed. I remember getting on the table and the doctor telling me he just needed to get a grip on the pin and it would be a quick removal. It may hurt some, he told me, but I was going to be OK, and it would be finished rather quickly. I remember my mom telling me to sit still so the doctor could take the pins out. My grandma told me it was going to be OK and to squeeze her hand tightly while the doctor removed the pins from my arm. The doctor prepped my arm and took out a shiny object to remove the pins. My grandma kept telling me I was going to be OK. The doctor gripped the pin and pulled it out, and blood started gushing out of my arm, and some flew across the room.

My grandmother started screaming and startled everyone in the room, and then she pounced on the doctor. "How could you do this to a little girl?" My grandmother had to leave the room for a few minutes because she was upset and kept yelling at the doctor. The doctor told my mom the assistants needed to bandage my arm. In the meantime, Mom was trying to calm my grandmother down in the hallway. After a few minutes, they both were finally able to come back in the room, and the doctor removed the final pin from my elbow. The doctor's assistant was holding my arm with pressure and talking calmly to me about my animals. The second pin was just as bloody and hurt just as bad while it was being removed. My grandmother was upset and started yelling at the doctor again about hurting her grandbaby. We finally were able to go home and put this behind us. In all honesty, I believe it hurt my grandmother more than it hurt me.

It took me a while to get back in the saddle again. Several times I recall my sister asking me to go with her on the horses. I always declined, and my dad heard me telling her I would not go with her again. He just shook his head and told me to get back on the horse and not be scared of falling again. "Be strong and Be courageous" (Joshua 1:9).

Finally I decided to start riding again. We had several rides and lots of fun on the horses. We would ride bareback on an old railroad track to the corner store. We would spend all day on the weekends just exploring the trails and seeing animals and plants along the way. We would race each other and set up logs for the horses to jump over.

This day, however, I was not on my horse; I was doubled up behind my sister riding on the same horse, and when we arrived home to complete the adventure, she went to dismount and told me to stay on the horse. I asked her, "How are you going to do that? I need to get down first." She told me again to stay on the horse. Well, she slung her leg back, her leg met my shoulder, and she kicked me off the horse. The force of her leg hitting me and Mother Earth's welcoming arms once again were not anything I want anyone to have to feel. My lungs were forced again to expel all the oxygen that they had held. Another trip to the hospital, to the place I did not want to go. After being held in that plastic cage without my family for so long, I was so scared I would have to be put back in again. I did not want to go, but my parents made me. I was hurting pretty bad, but this time it was in a different area. My body ached, and my right wrist hurt. This time it did not need a blood transfusion or surgery to repair. All it needed was a cast. I was thankful I did not have to stay overnight. My wrist was wrapped up in a cast, and I was sent home to heal. Even after break two, I still loved to ride horseback, and I know that you cannot let fear take over your life. Be a warrior not a worrier.

My childhood had plenty of adventures, happiness, and pain. "But he said to me, 'My grace is sufficient for you, for my power is made perfect in weakness.' Therefore I will boast all the more gladly about my weaknesses, so that Christ's power may rest on me. That is why, for Christ's sake, I delight in weaknesses, in insults, in hardships, in persecutions, in difficulties. For when I am weak, then I am strong" (2 Corinthians 12:9–10 [NIV]).

How do I begin to tell you about the tragic event that took place during my younger years? My aunt and uncle met me at my house when I was off the bus. At first I did not notice my parents were not around. I was happy that my cousins were there, and we started playing. My uncle Steve and aunt Ginny had been making dinner, and we all were told that my mom and dad were not going to be there for a while, that they would be taking care of us for a few days. We all were told to stay inside the house and keep the doors locked. My aunt and uncle had us all sit down and told us that something had happened to our grandma and both of my aunts. My mom's twin sister, her older sister, and their mother (my grandma) had all been murdered. My mom had found them murdered at her sister's house. The police and my dad were all talking, and a hunt was on for the murderer. My aunt hugged me and told me she would answer any questions and help me with anything I needed. A feeling of helplessness came over me, and I became distraught. I started crying and felt empty and did not understand how someone could do that. We had to keep the doors locked because the person was not caught and had taken all the children hostage. We did not know where he took all of the children, and we were scared for them. The next few months were awful, and it was filled with my mother crying. We all tried our best to help, though it was difficult. We missed our grandma and aunts deeply. Our lives had changed drastically in an instant.

"My soul is weary with sorrow; strengthen me according to your word" (Psalm 119:28).

As I was starting to adjust and grow into a young woman, my life as a child ended, and a young lady started to emerge. I was the youngest child of my family. My mother had been feeling ill for a few weeks and needed to go to the doctor. My mother found out why she had been ill and announced to us she was having a baby. This helped to lift our family out of the deep sadness we all had. The news of a new baby brought a new love and excitement to our lives. It was a very difficult time for my mother: she could hardly keep anything down and was sick all the time. She gave birth early, and the baby boy was on life support for several weeks. We were not sure if he was going to live. He was so tiny and frail, but he was getting stronger every day. We were finally able to take him home on heart monitors. With lots of love and care, he survived. I am forever grateful for the life and love he brought and still brings to our family. My parents named him Matthew, and he gave us new hope and a different focus than the grief of loss. My teen years consisted of helping with my little brother, attending new schools, and finding new friends.

Years passed and life happened. In my early twenties, I was married, and by my late twenties, I had my second child. I was overweight and unhappy. I had gained ninety to a hundred pounds per pregnancy and never lost it. I was struggling with my new role as a wife and mother of two boys. My husband traveled frequently for business. I hated where we lived, I hated the house, I hated the neighbors, I hated everything. My life was depressing for me. My husband would get home, and we would argue because my negative feelings would seep out. Yes, I became the energy zapper. I needed a change and begged my husband to move, and he declined. He told me there was no way in hell he was going to move. This house had been an amazing deal, and it also was directly across the street from my in-laws. The relationship was very toxic. My children were my top priority, and all I could focus on was them. I put my needs and my husband's last. I did not want to make him happy; why should I? I was miserable and begged for him to move several times. He was not home enough to listen or see how things really were. I kept shutting down my inner voice that screamed for change. I tried my best to be the perfect wife and mother. I was sad. I was hurting and was not listening to my body. I would tell myself, "Who cares? It doesn't matter." This is what a mother does: she takes care of everything for everyone else. So I became silent to my needs and only focused on others'.

"Let us not become weary in doing good, for at the proper time we will reap a harvest if we do not give up" (Galatians 6:9 [NIV]).

Fitness is about loving yourself. Fitness is loving the one body you have been given. It is about pouring sweat, living life, and feeling your heart beating. Loving your body and loving the skin you are in every day. It is not about looking better than someone or having more muscle. Fitness to me is about your own personal journey of health and happiness. I do not care if you wear makeup. Actually, I encourage you to wear makeup. It may sound vain to some; however, I know if I have to go somewhere without makeup, I don't want to go. So why would you want to put yourself in a compromised position and not wear makeup to begin with? Beats me! Fitness is about feeling alive and feeling better about your body. Fitness can be a form of detox or part of a recovery process. To me fitness is not about vanity. Fitness is about the internal person—the thoughts that start to become the choices, which in turn begin to be the discipline of a healthier person. Fitness is not always in the gym lifting weights. It is the healthy attitude and love for yourself. After all, your mind is a muscle as well.

My fitness story begins long before I stepped foot in a gym or lifted a weight. Many nights had passed when I knew I wanted to change myself. I was unhappy with my postbaby body; I ate anything and everything I wanted. I did not know how to change, and I could not quiet my inner thoughts. All I could think about was changing myself and my appearance. I hated looking at myself. I hated who I had become. I hated my surroundings. My life needed some sort of change. I begged my husband for change, and it was not happening. I had to do something to feel better and listen to the voice inside my head. I started to change my eating habits by limiting my food intake. I had no idea how to diet correctly, nor did I know anything about cardio or weightlifting. My diet consisted of water and bites of food here and there. I was limiting my intake drastically, basically starving myself. I was not doing any exercise. My head would hurt every day. I was not happy, and I did not feel well at all. My head would hurt so bad that I would lie down until the pain subsided. Then I would eat late at night and binge eat because I was so hungry. This was starting to take its toll on my body and my attitude.

My day started as it normally would—with getting my son to school—but my head hurt again, and this was the day my life changed *forever*. The next forty-eight hours are a blur. I remember seeing my son saying, "Mommy, Mommy," then strange men looking at me with a light in my face. I heard sirens and traffic and woke up in a strange, quiet room—white sheets pulled over me nice and snug. I looked over and seen beautiful long-stem yellow roses on a table. A TV in the corner with a dog show on. I frantically started looking around. I was not sure where I was or why. My arm was cold. I lifted it and seen I had something attached to it; it was an IV. A lady with dark hair walked into my room and asked me my name and SSN while looking at the bracelet on my arm. I was not sure of the answer. She asked me, "Do you know where you are?" I could barely talk; I could not think of how to communicate to her. I shook my head, confused and scared. She told me I was in a hospital and that she was my nurse. The next thing I remember is her telling me they are taking good care of me. I faded in and out of consciousness. This went on for days. I would awake to beeping and then a nurse giving me medication in my IV; then I would be asleep again. The nurse would ask me things when I woke up, but most I did not understand. I stopped trying to communicate and stopped trying to leave my bed. Several days passed and I could not talk. I didn't know how to express myself.

The next few days are a blur of waking to the sounds of clicking and people talking over my bed. When I awoke to a dark-haired man, he looked familiar. He asked me, "Do you know who I am?" I started to focus on his face; he looked familiar.

Right about that time the nurse walked in and told him, "Sir, visiting hours are over; she needs to rest." He requested to stay a few more minutes, but she declined and informed him of the times for visiting the next day.

My IV was taken out, and I started to stay awake for longer periods of time. I could not speak, I could not feed myself, and I did not know what was going on. I was being taken care of by hospital staff on all levels, and I needed full assisted care. Sometimes I would understand what they were saying, and other times it was like they were speaking a foreign language to me. The doctors told my parents and husband that I would never recover and that I would need to be put in an assisted-living facility for the remainder of my life. I did not understand or know what was happening to me. With every passing day, they lost hope in me as I seemed to be getting worse. I did not know how to communicate, dress, feed myself, comb my hair, or even walk to use the restroom. I could not recognize my family members or even my children.

Slowly my communication returned with broken words and sentences, but I started to speak again. I was tired of the room, tired of lying in bed. I wanted to get up and walk around. So I took the sheets off me and stood up beside my bed. My legs were like limp noodles and very weak. But I was determined to get out of that bed. I worked up enough strength to walk toward the door and out down the hallway to a window. It was dark outside, but as I arrived to the window, the sky was bright and so beautiful; I seen the outside world. A lady walked up behind me and said, "Hey there. What are you doing out of bed? Do you know where you are at?" I shook my head; I did not know.

I thought, *I must live close by.* Then I blurted out to her, "I must live close. I want to go home." She asked me where I lived. My reply was, "I don't know, but it must be close."

She told me, "You are *not* going to leave."

I started to press on the door, but it was locked. Anger filled me. *Why won't she let me leave?* I yelled at her, "*No*, I want to go home!"

121

She yelled for assistance, and then people started running toward me. I was so scared. They grabbed my arms, and one lady had a needle and jabbed my arm, and everything went dark.

Waking up was difficult. I did not know how long I had been sleeping. Every time I would wake up, I would try to get out of the bed. They had to put an alarm on my bed so when I moved or tried to get out, it would alert them. I was tied down, and every time I would wake up or try to get up, they would jab my arm with a needle to make me more controllable.

I finally stopped trying to move when I woke up. This time when my eyes opened, I lay very still and looked around the room. No one was in the room, and I started to look at the restraints along my body. I wanted to get out of the bed; I wanted to leave this place. My arm hurt from all the pricks, and my stomach was hurting. So many thoughts were in my head, so many things I did not understand. People talking to me, telling me to do certain things I did not understand. What I did understand was the pain of that needle being jabbed into my arm numerous times. I also understood the pain of the restraint across my chest and stomach. I kept looking at the straps and figured out a way to get loose from them. I tried several things to remove them, but my hands were strapped to the side of the bed. So I gently turned and tossed but being careful not to make the alarm go off. It took me a while, but I did it; I was out of the restraints. I lay in the bed for a while. I did not want that needle jabbed into my arm again. I just wanted to find the man whose face I found familiar a while ago. I wanted something to make sense to me. I was scared and wanted to leave. I knew I did not belong in that room.

The nurse walked in and found that I was out of my restraints. She asked me, "How did you manage to get out of them?"

I would not tell her, but I said, "They hurt. Leave them off."

Finally the nurse told me I was going to be able to leave the room. She informed me I would be going home with my mom and dad. She told me they were going to be able to take care of me. I was thrilled to be able to leave that room. The next few weeks were very difficult for everyone. I required full assistance with care and daily activities. I could not comb my hair, brush my teeth, or even tie my shoelaces. All daily objects were not recognizable. I did not know what to do with my spoon or even how feed myself. It was a slow process, but I started healing with the assistance of my family. I was like a toddler looking at the world again for the first time. My parents started to take me to the park, and they also would show me things and tell me what they did. My dad would point to stuff and read to me and play games to help me recall stuff. My husband brought me old magazines to look through. He also brought a book that was wrapped in cheetah print (my Bible). My husband would visit every few days. I knew he was my husband but did not want to go home with him right away. I was comfortable with my parents, but I was not allowed to see my children. My husband thought it would be best they did not see me in this condition.

Slowly my communication started to get better, and I started to recognize who they were. I flipped through magazines and seen weights and workouts and was trying to understand what they were doing. When we would walk in the park, I would try to do some things I had seen. One person I had seen while flipping through a magazine was Jennifer Nicole Lee. It was as if I gravitated to her pictures and wanted to do exactly what she does. Several months passed since I had begun going to the park with my parents, and they had started to see progress on basic daily activities. I was able to recognize a toothbrush, a hairbrush, a spoon, and a fork. I was starting to read more, and I was able to read my Bible. My husband would visit, and finally I was comfortable enough to go home, and he was comfortable to reunite me with my children. "Trust in the LORD with all your heart, And lean not on your own understanding; In all your ways acknowledge Him, And He shall direct your paths" (Proverbs 3:5–6 [NKJV]).

I loved being reunited with my children and my husband. However, I still had a long road to recovery. I did not have any memories that I could recall. The medical experts told me I had dementia and was still not fully capable of doing things on my own. They were not sure if it was from childhood injuries, like the numerous blows to my head from the falls at an early age. Or was it the drastic diet change? Was it from constant stress? The doctor's did not know what brought the dementia on. It was a struggle sometimes and very frustrating for me. My parents would pick me up every day, and we would go to different places. I would read my Bible and try to understand it. I would flip through magazines and find stuff I wanted to do. Finally I started to look up stuff on our home computer. My boys loved being on the computer, so they showed me how to do certain things, and I started navigating the computer when I had free time. I wanted to be better; I wanted to be stronger. I had lost weight in the hospital. And now I felt this energy and an inner voice directing me to that lady I seen in the magazine. I wanted to learn more about what she does and how she looks so healthy. I started to look for anything about her and what her program consisted of.

I also started doing stuff at the park with my parents. One day as we went for our walk, I wanted to run. So I started to run, and it felt amazing. My heart was beating fast, and I felt better after the run. After that day, all I could think about was going for a run and when I could work out again. My mom and my dad would get to the park and start walking, and I would just start running. I would run through the park breathing in the air, hearing the river rushing, seeing the Spanish moss blowing in the oak trees—it was just me and the trail. As I poured sweat and ran on that trail, more memories started to surface. My workouts consisted of me putting together what I had seen Jennifer Nicole Lee do in the magazine and what I could find online. I would write down what I had to do and go to the park. Some days I had to stay home because I couldn't drive yet. Those days I would have a makeshift track in my home. I would run around the entire bottom floor then up the flight of stairs, run down the stairs, then run back up again. I did not have any weights, so I pulled cans out of my pantry. I started doing the exercises with canned food. My mom had noticed I was doing this and bought me a pair of two-pound and four-pound weights at a yard sale and left them at my house. I was grateful and used the weights at the park and at home. The workouts and running gave me a new hope. I wanted to recall more memories, so I looked forward to waking up every morning. My life was being whispered gently to me while running. It was very emotional. It was my time to truly be alive, to feel my heart beating, to be pouring sweat, and to truly be thankful for a second chance at living my life. The workouts and running became my time with the Lord, my time to remember. Days passed, and I kept doing the workouts. I would drop my oldest off at school and take my little one to the park. I would work out and run while he rode his bike beside me. As I would run or work out, that little voice inside kept getting stronger. My family and my husband noticed how much stronger I had become. Not physically but mentally stronger. I started to become more independent and able to do normal daily activities again. I started to communicate better and make decisions for myself and my children.

"God is within her, she will not fail" (Psalms 46:5).

Finally, after a slow recovery process, I started to look for ways to improve my mind and health. I found Tosca Reno and her clean-eating plan, so I eliminated sugar from my diet. I started to engross myself in fitness and health. Again I saw this lady's face, the lady who had planted the seed of fitness into my soul. It was Jennifer Nicole Lee on the cover of *Oxygen Magazine*. I tore open the magazine and was excited to read about her. I found her on social media and seen she had contact information. She was looking for fitness models and stories of success. I thought, *This is it. I need to write to her and tell her how she has helped me to recover.* It took a few days to get up the nerve and courage to be able to tell my story. It is still very difficult to divulge. I am forever grateful for her workouts and my strength to continue every day. Her message and inspirational words help you through the workouts. Not only has she helped me heal, but she has helped me to be mentally fit. I was honored when she called me and did a phone interview, and on that call she asked me to attend her Fitness Model Factory event in New York City. Overjoyed and in disbelief, I began to prepare for the event. I had an amazing time and cannot explain the powerful positive vibes that it left me with.

After a few months of being home, I wanted to attend college and get a degree in exercise. A few people questioned me with setting these goals. I didn't listen; I wanted to push my mind. I also wanted to have more knowledge about being able to help other people exercise. I am happy to say I now hold an ACE (American Council on Exercise) certificate.

I have been involved with JNL for years now and have attended many events with her in Miami and New York City. The people involved with JNL are strong, positive individuals. They are men and women with a message. A movement of raw, real beauty. We all have flaws, and flaws are beautiful. We all have them, but it depends on what you call a flaw. It may be a freckle, a scar, big curly hair, thin hair, or even stretch marks. Or even emotional baggage. You must find the inner peace to be who you are as an individual. To be comfortable in your own skin again. The daily stress you may have can be released through your workouts. This helps to ensure your health and mind remain vibrant.

I will continue to move forward. I will always look for the positive in any situation no matter how difficult. I see my life as a way to inspire others and be a light of hope. I found new meaning and appreciation for the small things in life. I am not into fitness for vanity by any means. I am into fitness for my mind, health, and happiness. It is my hope that I will not have to face dementia again in my old age, for dealing with dementia the first time was difficult enough. I promised myself I would make every moment count while I could remember and along the way make the most incredible memories. I know a small fraction of my life will forever be in this book and hope to inspire countless others.

Find your joy every day. It can and will transform your mind and life. Make every moment count.

Candi Nicole Taylor

CHAPTER FOURTEEN

Giselle D. Martinez

From Victim to Victorious

First off, I would like to start off by thanking Jennifer Nicole Lee for granting me the opportunity to share this story through this outlet. Secondly, I would like to thank my parents and close friends for their endless support, and lastly, I would like to tell everyone (male or female) that there's always a light at the end of the tunnel (no matter how bleak it may seem).

My story starts off like every other relationship story: boy meets girl. I had met my ex-boyfriend in my organic chemistry class. He was the shy type, always serious, diligent in class, and cute to boot. So when I asked him if I could join his study group, I was beyond peachy at the fact that I would be able to kill two birds with one stone: 1) spend time with a guy who I obviously thought was cute and 2) study for my organic chemistry course. In the upcoming weeks, as time would have it, we grew closer, and the text messaging became more frequent between the two of us. He finally asked me out on a date, and we met up at a sushi bar.

The date was as painfully awkward as one could imagine it to be, and his shyness (while cute) made the situation even more so. So I did what I did best and started talking. I slowly eased him into conversation, and we ended up talking until the restaurant closed. Shortly after he walked me to my car, he said, "I'm honestly surprised that this date went so well. I always thought that you were annoying and horribly loud, but I'm pleasantly surprised that you know how to behave." My initial reaction was to laugh because I thought that he was being sarcastic. Little did I know that this was only the beginning, and that was a red flag I completely ignored.

As we started dating, his comments started becoming a bit more abusive. From "I don't like it when you put on makeup; you look ridiculous," to "I don't like it when you do your nails." They continued to pour out of his mouth, and my inexperience in relationships at that time told me that, as a "good" girlfriend, I should listen to all his grievances and do what he wanted me to do to fix the problem. So I did just that. I stopped wearing makeup, doing my nails, wearing "provocative" clothing (I couldn't wear yoga leggings because other men would look at me), wearing heels, and doing my hair (for the same reason as to why I had to stop wearing the leggings). I also couldn't perform anymore (I had been involved in musical theater and dance since I was a small child), and most of all, I couldn't talk to my friends because he didn't approve of them.

My parents started noticing that my aura had changed. I was no longer happy, and everything I did for that relationship was taxing me to no end. But whenever I was told that I should break up with him, whether it be by my parents or a close friend, I would just break down crying because I couldn't...or rather, because I was scared to do so. My self-esteem had been broken down so severely that I had begun to think that I *needed* to be with him, as most of my friends didn't want to be around me because they would see how sad I was becoming, and I had been brainwashed to believe that my parents didn't hold my best interest at heart. Needless to say, I had isolated myself from all the people who cared about me, and this put me in a worse situation both mentally and emotionally.

The fights became more verbally abusive. Not only that, but he had begun to fight with me in public. One specific fight occurred at a Subway close to my university. We were waiting in line, and I had noticed that the girl standing in front of me looked familiar. Once she turned around, we immediately recognized each other and started catching up as the last time we had seen each other had been in a high school English course. The line started progressing rather quickly because, for once, I felt as if I was "free" in a sense. But that freedom was short-lived. During our conversation over what majors we were both studying, my boyfriend loudly sneered, "God, you never fucking stop talking."

My friend had caught the comment and looked at him before looking at me. I could feel my face turning beet red in embarrassment as he turned around and loudly commented to one of his friends behind him how he should find a muzzle for me because I didn't know how to shut up. While this was occurring, I quickly told my friend that my boyfriend had a weird sense of humor that seemed insulting to some, but it was genuinely coming from a good place without malice. I began to laugh nervously, but she wasn't buying it, and she proceeded to turn around and walk forward in line. I became quiet. I didn't want to upset him, so I didn't speak at all. Once our turn in line came up, I asked him what he wanted on his sandwich, and he told me, "What I always get," rather snarkily.

I took a deep breath, smiled, and proceeded to give the order to the guy working upfront. We got to the toppings, and the man preparing the sandwich asked me if I wanted jalapeños on my boyfriend's sandwich. Although I knew that he always had a tendency of putting jalapeños on his sandwiches, he hadn't been doing so as of late because of heartburn issues. So I wanted to make sure, and I gently asked him if he wanted jalapeños on his sandwich. He screamed at me, "*Didn't I fucking tell you yes?*"

The man preparing the sandwich froze, as did everyone else in the store, but no one did anything—no one stood up and said something, which became a rather typical occurrence for me whenever he yelled at me in public. I quickly regained my composure, smiled, and told the sandwich man, "Thank you," before turning to my boyfriend and telling him that I needed to use the restroom. It took every bit of strength inside me to walk to the bathroom without falling apart, and it was upon entering a stall that I truly poured my eyes out crying. I couldn't continue living like this. It was progressively getting worse, and everything was *always my fault*. There couldn't possibly be so many things that were wrong with me—I couldn't be *that* insufferable. I needed a way out, but that wasn't going to occur for another six months.

The fights progressively got worse, and I became more introverted as the relationship continued. Then, one day, I just couldn't take it anymore. The fight that day started like every typical fight in that relationship: I had done something wrong and bothered him. We were studying, and I was using a pen that you had to push in the back in order to use. I decided to use the table to gently push in the backs on the three pens I was using so that I could change the colors.

I was immediately told that I was being loud and inconsiderate, that I always found a way to be annoying, and that I could never just behave. At that point, when he started his rant, I had had it. I began to slowly pack my stuff up into my backpack as his tone continued to increase. I slowly got up, slid my backpack straps onto my shoulders, and walked toward the door. I began to hear distant footsteps followed by loud "heys," but I didn't turn back. My goal was to reach that doorknob, my car, my house.

As I was reaching out to grab the knob, I felt a hand on the back of my neck followed by a very strong pull that knocked me off balance. I almost fell on my back, but I managed to spin and land on my feet. I was facing him as he said, "I'm not done with you." I immediately saw my life flash before my eyes. It couldn't end like this—it just couldn't—and if no one was going to fight for me, then Goddamn it, I was! I immediately pushed him back and punched him in the nose, and I said, "Don't you *ever* touch me like that or it will be the last time you ever touch anyone." I quickly grabbed the doorknob and sprinted to my car before speeding off home.

I sobbed the entire way there. Although I knew that I had finally fought back, I still felt as if I had lost because I had let so much happen to me at the hands of this man. I had lost my self-esteem and my confidence, and I had gone into depression. I was embarrassed that I had let it all happen, that I had become a victim...

It took several months of therapy and self-help to rebuild my self-esteem, to rebuild my confidence, and to not be ashamed that I was a victim. I managed to survive, to leave, to fight back, while many other people are still in that toxic situation. So I'm here to tell you that you are strong! That you *can* overcome your abusive situation! And that you *can fight back*! Don't ever take anything from anyone, don't ever let anyone tell you you're less than what you are, don't ever be scared to speak out about your situation, don't ever be scared to seek help, and most importantly don't ever let anyone take your happiness away.

May my story be an inspiration to others going through the same thing, and may my story serve as a template for others to overcome seemingly arduous obstacles.

—Giselle D. Martinez

CHAPTER FIFTEEN

Mary Fredrickson

My Journey From Health Scare to
Super-Fit Mom of Eleven Kids

I am a mom of eleven kids, and yes I gave birth to all those delight-ful kiddos. And yes they are all a result of my wonderful husband of twenty-four years and I. I have always been a pretty active mom, and became even more active during my pregnancies to avoid gain-ing too much weight, which was usually around 35-40 pounds. After each baby, I would focus on losing the baby weight with the goal of fitting back in those pre-pregnancy jeans. My husband got involved in my personal weight loss contests by paying $100 per child when I reached my goal. Imagine my payout after the eleventh child...yes $1100!

As if being a busy mom wasn't enough, I experienced a series of setbacks that got me in a rut. Five years ago my dear father was taken from this earth swiftly after being diagnosed with pancreatic cancer. I was fortunate enough to spend many precious days with him before he was gone, and I realized how quickly a loved one can be lost. A few months later I began training for a half-marathon to help cope with my loss. During my training, my knee was injured, and I had to cease my running immediately. My knee continued to get worse and would become dislocated without warning. I was limited to walking for lower body exercises. I then discovered I was pregnant with my tenth child, and I was unable to be as active as I was during past pregnancies. This was depressing as I felt more tired and not as energetic as I felt when I was more active with previous pregnancies. I discovered JNL on YouTube and found her to be upbeat and motivating. I continued listening to her motivating talks while walking my way through my pregnancy.

The day before Thanksgiving, we welcomed into our family our fourth healthy boy. Although having a large family can sometimes be challenging and feel overwhelming, we have been blessed with healthy active children. When Christmas arrived at our home I was overwhelmed with joy when I discovered my wonderful and supportive husband had ordered me the JNL Fusion DVD workout program. This program was just what I needed at the time. As soon as I was cleared by my doctor to start working out, I began the workout program and followed her advice on modifying the workout to accommodate limitations, in my case my bad knee. I was able to "earn my shower" as she always says.

After struggling with my knee for a year, I was told by a doctor surgery was necessary to repair it. After completing physical therapy, I was cleared to start light training and was excited about getting back into my fitness routine. Yet, it was not to be. On Thanksgiving Day, I was walking down a flight of stairs carrying my one-year old baby. My knee gave out and I used my left arm to break the fall. Unfortunately, this fall dislocated my left shoulder. This was the worst pain I have ever experienced. If you have never experienced the pain of having a shoulder dislocated, I can tell you it was worse for me than giving natural child birth, which I have done five times. After spending another Thanksgiving Day in the hospital, I returned home and found myself back at the physical therapist for another round of treatment.

I became more interested in fitness and started a personal trainer certification program. I also attended a fitness exposition and met a personal trainer who has six kids and is in great shape. I started training with her and I have learned so much about fitness from JNL and my personal trainer. They have both been so inspirational in my fitness journey!

In early spring I became pregnant with our eleventh child. Shortly after becoming pregnant, my sister was diagnosed with cancer on Mother's Day. I was very close to my sister and took the news hard. She was like a best friend and the one person other than my husband that I could share anything with. When I was feeling down, she cheered me up.

On Thanksgiving Day, I once again found myself in the hospital. This time it was to bring into the world our seventh daughter. She came earlier than expected, but was a healthy energetic baby. I was starting to wonder if I would ever spend a normal Thanksgiving again!

The following summer, my dear sister succumbed to the cancer that ravaged her body for two years. The year following her death was difficult on all the first anniversaries such as Mother's Day, my sister's birthday, and the anniversary of her death. During these up and down times in my life, I had continued to do JNL Fusion workouts 3-5 times a week. These workouts helped me stay strong, energetic, and positive.

The cancer related deaths of my father and sister caused me to look at my own health situation more closely. Diabetes, high blood pressure, and cancer are apparent in my family history. During a couple of my pregnancies I had borderline gestational diabetes and I was told by the nurse that if I wanted to avoid getting diabetes when I got older I would have to exercise at least 5 days a week. The fitness lifestyle has become a part of our entire family for our overall health and wellbeing. I find this healthy lifestyle so important that a couple years ago I became a certified personal trainer to help others, especially mothers, learn about the value of a healthy lifestyle.

My life experiences have taught me that life is a series of ups and downs. I also believe that God gives us trials for a reason, and overcoming these challenges makes us stronger. JNL provided me the "Jolt" in my life when I really needed it! Fitness has now become a lifestyle rather than the destination of just fitting in my jeans after having a baby. No matter how busy your life is, you can always find ways to incorporate fitness into your lifestyle. You do not have to spend hours in the gym to get results. Being active helps you mentally and physically to be a better person. I continue to train weekly in the gym with my husband, see my personal trainer, and get my Jolt of JNL in at home.

A couple years ago I put a photo of JNL on my vision board. She had signed the photo "Mary, I believe in you!" which I had received in a contest she had done. Just recently I was able to achieve my dream of meeting JNL in her fitness studio and training with her one-on-one. Meeting her was a great experience and she was everything I imagined her to be and more! Thank you JNL!

CHAPTER SIXTEEN

Michelle Diaz

Create Your Own Role, Play Your Own Part, Be Comfortable in Your Own Skin, and Believe in Yourself

When I was fifteen years old, I discovered my passion for singing, creating art, and making music. Today I keep that passion alive through the local music empire I strived to create with my partner, Madison Coviello. At the age of nineteen, I started college at Full Sail University, earning my bachelor of science degree in recording arts in just twenty-two months. When I met Madison nearly a year ago, we quickly realized our passions took similar paths and decided to work together as Viper and Piper to bring our love for creativity and artistic expression to Orlando. Together we created a local arts collective in collaboration with III Points Music Festival, a music, art, and technology event at Mana in Wynwood, Miami. We held our event, Viper x Piper's Trinity Temple Music Festival with "on the road to III Points," at Woodstock Orlando and treated attendees to a new dimension of artistic experience with live performances, music, and art in which we created the power of three to go along with the III Points brand. This is how we made our slogan: "First you will self-destruct. Then you will be reborn. Here are your third eyes. Now come tribe with us." The theme of our festival was to go through the three portals of creation, destruction, and rebirth. Altogether we had more than four hundred people attend our first event, including top artists from Miami, Los Angeles, New York, Orlando, and even France. We also had live performers such as our white witches decorating people to their higher selves as well as live artist painting and projection mapping.

As a nearly twenty-one-year-old graduate, I have designed, built, and produced my own music and arts festival with the help of my partner, Piper. Taking on monumental roles of responsibility, we prepared and presented numerous project proposals dictating ideas, budgets, and plans. We handpicked each artist who would perform or be exhibited. We oversaw the logistics and technicalities from start to finish, smoothing out the bumps along the way, managing and directing every artist and crew member. We poured our heart and soul into Trinity Temple in order to ensure a successfully inclusive and diverse event that collectively celebrated music, art, and community.

This is just the beginning of my career as an artist, and the connections I've made and the support I've received have been invaluable. While Trinity Temple was definitely a learning experience, it was one that gave me the drive to pursue my passion and move forward. My purpose in life is to create and inspire, promote and encourage artistic expression, and bring people together through the beauty of art and music. I do not categorize myself as any one thing, and I do not let the opinions of others keep me from doing what I love or expressing my individuality. I will continue to be who I am, no matter what anyone else says. Don't ever let anyone tell you that you can't do it or that you don't look the part. Make your own part, play your own role, and be whatever you want to be because in the end, the most important thing is being comfortable in your own skin and believing in yourself.

—Michelle Diaz

CHAPTER SEVENTEEN

Katherine Streeton

My Journey from Unbalanced DIE-t to
Living a Balanced, Healthy Lifestyle

I remember going on my first diet. All I wanted was to lose a few pounds. I started eating less and exercising more. No big deal, right?

I was fourteen years old. I had no idea at the time that this would be the beginning of more than a decade of eating disorders. Nor did I know that the word *diet* is spelled DIE-t for a reason!

Everyone has heard of anorexia and bulimia, but orthorexia is a little less known. Wikipedia defines orthorexia as an extreme or excessive preoccupation with eating food believed to be healthy. The difficult thing about it is where you draw the line between healthy eating and exercise and an obsession over every piece of food that goes into your mouth. How do you recognize when somebody you care about has orthorexia when on the outside all he or she appears to be doing is making lifestyle improvements?

Maybe my story will provide some insight. For whatever reason, when I was around thirteen or fourteen years old, I got the idea in my head that I was fat and that I needed to lose weight. I remember reading a fictional book about a girl who, in an attempt to lose weight, started to swim each day. What a great idea, I thought. My school was located right next to a swimming center. I woke up at five o'clock each morning to swim for an hour before going to school. There is nothing wrong with this per se, but I didn't particularly enjoy swimming, nor did I have any intentions of making it a career or competing in the sport. I just saw it as a way to burn calories.

Regarding food, I had an idea in my mind of what constituted as healthy and what didn't. For an entire year, I wouldn't touch anything that I didn't consider to be healthy. Soon after I went on my diet, I became severely depressed. It's hard to say which came first, the chicken or the egg (in this case my eating disorder or my depression), but all I know is that it wasn't a pretty time in my life.

I found comfort in food, and this led me to another extreme: binge eating disorder. I used food to fill a void deep inside me. Because I had been depriving myself of anything "unhealthy" for so long, the first bite of food that was high in fat, sugar, and salt was a big deal for me. I asked myself what I had been missing out on for so long. I was so depressed that I momentarily put my desire to be skinny on the side. The food I had been depriving myself of tasted too good. After all, one chocolate bar is not going to make that much of a difference in the end, is it?

For one month I bought a two-hundred-gram chocolate bar every day after school and ate the whole bar in one go. I was too embarrassed to go to the same supermarket each day to buy my chocolate, so some days I would walk a little bit farther to a store where I wasn't a regular customer.

The weight started to slowly creep on. I pretended not to notice. After a month of my chocolate diet, you could really tell the difference in my appearance.

It wasn't until a regular check-up with my high school nurse, however, that I was confronted with the truth about my weight. The nurse told me, "You know you are carrying some extra weight, don't you? This is a good thing, though, as it means you will have a regular period." (Haha, not quite. More about this later in my story.)

By the time I was seventeen, I was cycling between a very strict diet (i.e., starving myself) and binging on food. I hated my body. Exercise was a form of punishment for me and just an attempt to burn the calories I had consumed after losing control of my eating.

I was able to hide my eating disorder from everyone else. Because I cycled between dieting and binging, my weight didn't fluctuate too much. Whenever I lost a bit of weight on a diet, it would come back because I never made any permanent habit changes. I was riding a roller coaster of losing and gaining weight, dieting and binging. There seemed to be no end to it nor any way out.

One day when I was in my midtwenties, I remember seeing an infomercial with a beautiful woman in it. She radiated health and positive energy. Her name was Jennifer Nicole Lee. I thought I wanted to be just like her.

Soon after this day, there came a turning point in my fitness journey. I made a decision that would change my life. I was in Los Angeles, California. It was a beautiful summer's day, and I was by the swimming pool with a colleague of mine. At this point I was an international air hostess traveling around the world and living a dream. I was twenty-six years old.

It was a hot day, and I was wearing a bikini underneath my clothes. I thought about removing my clothes so I could fully enjoy the rays of the sun on my body.

But the shame I felt about the way I looked was stronger than my desire not to care about other people's opinions. I kept my clothes on. When I went back to my hotel room, I removed my clothes, and I was left standing in front of a mirror in my bikini. This was the moment I took my before photo, remembering the infamous before photo of Jennifer Nicole Lee. This would be mine. This would be the first day of a new chapter in my life. And it was.

The mind really is the most powerful muscle in the human body. No change can occur until you make the decision to change and not let anything stop you.

Once you make the decision to change, you need to take action. I ordered a home fitness DVD program and committed myself to completing it.

Within just a couple of months, I saw huge changes in my body. I made small changes to the way I ate, and I did *not* deprive myself nor restrict the amount of calories I consumed. I was in no rush to lose weight; all I was concerned about was making a permanent change in my appearance and confidence.

After a few months of exercising at home, I knew I needed to do something different. I hired a personal trainer to teach me how to lift weights. He told me I was his most motivated client. I spent all my free time reading about training and nutrition. My life had completely transformed.

Eventually, I made the decision to become a certified personal trainer myself so that I could share my passion and help other people. I was still working full-time as a flight attendant, so I spent all my spare time attending classes and studying for the Certified Personal Trainer exam.

I passed the exam and was one of the top students in my class. I was now a CPT, had the body I used to visualize myself having, was in a loving relationship, and was living abroad and traveling the world. My life should have been perfect now, right?

It was except for one thing: I was experiencing severe bloating, which really affected my self-esteem. It didn't make any sense. I was taking care of my body. I was eating healthily and exercising daily. Why was I bloated so often?

I went to see a nurse about my bloating. She asked me whether I had a regular period. I wondered what that had to do with my bloating. I replied that I had never had a regular period. I had run some tests a few years earlier to try to find the reason behind my irregular period, and the gynecologist hadn't found anything wrong with me.

The nurse told me she suspected I had PCOS or polycystic ovary syndrome. What is that?

I learned that it's a hormonal imbalance. Women with PCOS produce more androgen, which is a male hormone. One of the biggest complications is difficulty getting pregnant as a result of an irregular, or in some cases missing, period.

Some of the side effects include acne, hirsutism (excessive hair growth), and bloating. Unfortunately, there is no cure for PCOS, only a way to treat the symptoms. The most common treatment is the birth control pill, which is a synthetic form of estrogen, the female hormone responsible for regulating the period.

A lot of women with PCOS are either overweight or have a hard time losing weight, and my doctor told me bloating was one of the symptoms I would just have to live with.

There are days that I really struggle with my self-esteem. The best way for women with PCOS to manage their symptoms is through a healthy lifestyle. This includes a diet low on the glycemic index and regular exercise. Luckily, by the time I was diagnosed, I had already made exercise a habit. I actually look forward to my training on most days.

Exercise will help keep your weight under control and assist the weight-loss process for those who need it. (If you have PCOS, one of the best things you can do is get your weight within a healthy range.) For me, however, the best thing about exercise is how it affects my mood. It is known that our bodies release endorphins (or feel-good hormones) during exercise.

I used to have aesthetic goals, and I was striving to look a certain way for almost my entire adult life and throughout my teens. The truth is that none of us can control the number on the scale each morning. None of us can control the insertion and origin of our muscles or how our abs will look after cutting down to a low body-fat percentage. If I based my self-worth on the image I see in the mirror each day, then my happiness and self-esteem would be out of my control.

What if, instead, we were to set performance goals in the gym such as getting stronger, running faster, jumping higher, or lifting more weight? Wouldn't that be more empowering?

Shifting my own training goals from how I look to how my body performs has literally saved me. It gives me the ability to be happy every day regardless of whether I am bloated at that time.

Each day we have a choice to make. I choose to show up and train on most days because it makes me feel good. I choose to eat healthy foods after I indulge on occasion. I choose not to beat myself up when I'm not perfect.

What choices will you make starting today?

Katherine is a personal trainer, SFG level 1 kettlebell instructor, specialist in fitness nutrition, and makeup artist who is passionate about empowering women to feel more confident and beautiful in their skin. She creates customized training programs and meal plans through her online training site. Katherine can be reached at katherine@katherine.streeton.com *and* www.katherinestreeton.com.

ABOUT JENNIFER NICOLE LEE

Jennifer Nicole Lee is a "Lifestyle Strategist" coaching people around the world on how to create more success in their lives, through a mind, body and soul approach. Her own personal weight loss success is a direct result of her very own principles that she now teaches around the world. She is the best selling autahor of numerous books geared towards helping all create their dream lifestyle. She is the owner of her e-Classroom, where she teaches live interactive workouts, hosts educational webinars, & empowers all of her VIP clients in her coaching calls & consultations at www.JNLFitnessStudioOnline. com Her main website www.JenniferNicoleLee.com offers tons of motivation, inspiration & support for all looking to increase the quality of their lifestyle.

If you have a motivational story you would like to share in JNL's Volume 3 of "Motivational Kick in the Butt", please submit your story to TheJenniferNicoleLee@gmail.com

For additional coaching, online training, and lifestyle strategy webinars, please visit www.JNLFitnessStudioOnline.com

Made in the USA
Lexington, KY
27 June 2017